MODERN GERMAN AUTHORS
New Series

EDITED BY R. W. LAST

VOLUME SIX

SIEGFRIED LENZ

by

BRIAN MURDOCH and MALCOLM READ

OSWALD WOLFF

London

MODERN GERMAN AUTHORS—New Series
ed. R. W. Last

British Library Cataloguing in Publication Data

Murdoch, Brian
   Siegfried Lenz. — (Modern German authors: new series; vol. 6).
   1. Lenz, Siegfried — Criticism and interpretation
   I. Title   II. Read, Malcolm   III. Series
   833'.9'14   PT2623.E583Z/

   ISBN 0–85496–068–6
   ISBN 0–85496–069–4 Pbk

                    ISBN Cloth 0 85496 068 6
                         Paper 0 85496 069 4

                © 1978 Oswald Wolff (Publishers) Limited
                         London W1M 6DR

                MADE AND PRINTED IN GREAT BRITAIN BY
                    THE GARDEN CITY PRESS LIMITED
                    LETCHWORTH, HERTFORDSHIRE
                            SG6 1JS

CONTENTS

INTRODUCTORY NOTE

Citation from Lenz's work is problematic because many of his writings have appeared in a variety of hardback and paperback editions. Since it is impossible to please everybody, we have decided wherever possible to quote from the paperback edition of the works. These are usually published by the Deutscher Taschenbuchverlag (DTV); where there is no such edition, we have quoted from the standard hardback edition, usually published by Hoffmann and Campe. Abbreviated titles are as follows, and full bibliographical details and dates of alternative editions as well as those listed here may be found in the final bibliography.

Aug. *Die Augenbinde. Nicht alle Förster sind froh* (Rowohlt)
Bez. *Beziehungen* (DTV)
Brot. *Brot und Spiele* (DTV)
D. *Deutschstunde* (DTV)
Duell. *Duell mit dem Schatten* (Hoffmann und Campe)
Ein. *Einstein überquert die Elbe bei Hamburg. Erzählungen* (Hoffmann und Campe)
Fs. *Das Feuerschiff. Erzählungen* (DTV)
GdM. *Der Geist der Mirabelle* (Hoffmann und Campe)
Ges. *Das Gesicht* (Hoffmann und Campe)
Hab. *Es waren Habichte in der Luft* (DTV)
Haus. *Haussuchung. Hörspiele* (DTV)
JdS. *Jäger des Spotts. Geschichten aus dieser Zeit* (DTV)
Leh. *Lehmanns Erzählungen* (Hoffmann und Campe)
LvH. *Leute von Hamburg* (Hoffmann und Campe)
Mann. *Der Mann im Strom* (DTV)
Stg. *Stadtgespräch* (DTV)

Sul. *So zärtlich war Suleyken* (Fischer)
Sv. *Der Spielverderber. Erzählungen* (DTV)
Vor. *Das Vorbild* (Hoffmann und Campe)
ZdS. *Zeit der Schuldlosen* (Kiepenheuer und Witsch)

All translations quoted in the body of the text are our own.

1

SIEGFRIED LENZ

The literary-minded visitor to Germany in 1976 could not but be struck by the frequency of displays in bookshop windows celebrating the fiftieth birthday of Siegfried Lenz. The impression gained—quite correctly—was of a highly successful and popular writer. That the celebration was of Lenz's fiftieth and not, say, his seventieth year might have caused the uninformed to speculate, given the variety of volumes available, as to whether Lenz had embarked early on his career as an author, or whether he had been more than usually prolific. Both conclusions are correct, in fact. The assessment of Lenz's work, therefore, brings with it several difficulties. There is, one assumes, more to come, perhaps much more, and these future productions may be very varied. Any study of this sort must necessarily be in the nature of an interim report. This is perhaps heightened in the case of a writer who is enjoying at the moment a *popular* prestige, with its attendant exposure.

Lenz's first book appeared when he was twenty-five, the novel *Es waren Habichte in der Luft* (There were Hawks in the Sky, 1951). Since then, six other novels have appeared. The last but one of these, *Deutschstunde* (The German Lesson, 1968) established him as a novelist of world importance. The attention of the literary public in Germany was first caught, however, not by one of these novels, but by a selection of short stories recalling life in Lenz's birthplace, Masuria. These stories, which centre around the imaginary village of Suleyken in what was formerly East Prussia but which is now part of Poland, appeared in 1955 under the title *So zärtlich war Suleyken* (How Sweet was Suleyken), and have been popular

9

ever since. Other volumes of short stories have since appeared, either with a unified theme like the Suleyken tales, or collected from his large output of short stories in journals and newspapers. Many stories remain uncollected. A third field in which Lenz has made a mark is that of the radio play, most notably with his drama *Zeit der Schuldlosen—Zeit der Schuldigen* (Time of the Innocents—Time of the Guilty, 1960/61).

Lenz's range goes beyond these genres, however. He has published numerous essays of a literary-critical nature, and made contributions to all kinds of publications: for example, a short story (published originally in a periodical) is included in a collection called *Begegnungen mit Tieren* (Encounters with Animals, 1972), and Lenz's contribution has been interestingly, but not unexpectedly, reissued in textbooks for students of German. In collaboration, Lenz has edited the writings of a nineteenth-century satirist, and has provided the commentary to commercial travel books. Other collections are difficult to categorise, and his *Leute von Hamburg* (People of Hamburg, 1968) is a case in point, although Lenz has produced besides these a variety of other pen-portraits of Hamburg, its people and its harbour, and this could almost be counted as a genre in itself. There are, finally, some fairly modest political statements, and a large number of interviews. It might also be added that Lenz's works have often appeared in a series of different versions, frequently beginning as radio talks or features before their appearance in print.

Lenz's career, then, has covered enough time and has been productive enough for judgements to be made with a certain degree of confidence. Given the output, it is not surprising to learn that Lenz's early career should have embraced journalism (on *Die Welt* just after the war) and that Lenz should have referred several times since to this as a kind of literary apprenticeship.

Nor is there any shortage of secondary material, although it has shown a tendency towards repetition and unjustifiable but frequent reprinting. For all that, it gives further indication of the writer's popularity—as indeed does his appearance as the subject both of the doctoral dissertation and the school or university reader. Since 1973, at least four general surveys of Lenz's life and works have appeared and the number of monographs dealing with individual works or themes is similarly on the increase. He has, finally, also been awarded a number of literary prizes, some of which have occasioned speeches—one on 'Competition between Unequals' (Der Wettlauf der Ungleichen) on the position of the writer in a scientific age, given when he received the German Masonic Literary Prize in May 1970.[1] He has also been a member of the influential literary *Gruppe 47*.

The printing history of some of Lenz's works can be enlightening. Most of the novels appeared first in hardback editions with Hoffmann and Campe in Hamburg. (Lenz has, indeed, written a small appreciation of the house which did—interestingly—publish a 'prospectus' of extracts and summaries of his work.) Of the five earliest novels, four have recently been reprinted in a single volume. All but one of the novels down to *Deutschstunde* have appeared in paperback, as indeed have most of the short-story collections. *Deutschstunde* had sold approaching a million copies by the time *Das Vorbild* (An Exemplary Life, 1973) was published, and twenty-one foreign licences had been issued for versions of it in a variety of languages. By 1974 it had even appeared in the GDR, and the television film had been sold to twelve countries. *Das Vorbild*, which appeared first as a serial in the *Frankfurter Allgemeine Zeitung*, had sold a quarter of a million copies within the first four months of its appearance in book form.[2] Other works have been filmed or televised, and translations (though not in English) are numerous, as are book club editions of individual works.

The details of Siegfried Lenz's life are by no means obscure: indeed, the very degree to which Lenz has been exposed as a person to the reading public is worthy of comment, although this is connected with the rôle imputed to the writer

11

in West Germany today as a kind of mentor or professional commentator. Lenz has written two sketches of his life, both of which have been reprinted (in gradually updated forms) several times. The first, his 'Autobiographische Skizze' (Autobiographical Sketch) appeared originally in 1962, the second, 'Ich zum Beispiel—Kennzeichen eines Jahrgangs' (Myself for Example—Profile of an Age-Group) in 1966.[3] He has also commented frequently on his work (and German writers as a whole have been inclined, perhaps more frequently than their English-language counterparts, to publish details of the genesis of individual texts), and has discussed too his literary models and influences. And if the charge may be levelled that in all these writings Lenz is being subjectively selective, then it is worth noting that a large number of 'Interviews with Siegfried Lenz' have also appeared, often after broadcast versions. All this exposure goes far beyond the biographical brevity of the notes on the back of the DTV paperbacks, yet it is again an interesting modern phenomenon that the details there are presented to the maximum number of readers in a memorably succinct form. It is, then, well-nigh impossible to divorce details of a writer's life from his writings. Nor is it likely that Lenz would wish us to do so. The imaginary Suleyken is accompanied, for example, by an afterword discussing the *real* Masuria in the period before the last war.

Lenz was born in 1926 in what was then the southern part of East Prussia, now Polish Masuria, in the town now called Elk, then called Lyck, which is surrounded by lakes and relatively remote from other large centres. Lenz has written a number of essays about Lyck and the people of Masuria, and the origins of the Suleyken tales have been noted. Lenz grew up in the atmosphere of Nazi Germany, for all the remoteness of the area, was six when Hitler came to power, and nineteen when the war ended. In 'Ich zum Beispiel' Lenz speaks of his 'outer obedience' (Bez., p. 14), and he accepted the coming of the war with little more than curiosity, seeing himself (significantly for his later work) as 'indispensable as a spectator' (Bez., p. 15), and as a witness. At the same time, though, he was urged by a schoolmaster to read novelists who 'proclaimed man's inability to cope with the world' (Bez., p. 17).

At seventeen, Lenz was drafted fairly precipitously into the navy and he experienced the later part of the war at first hand. He heard of the assassination attempt on Hitler, an incident that he recalls (perhaps a little predictably) as giving him in retrospect the idea that collective obedience is an impossibility, a theme to which he (as others) was to return. At the end of the war he deserted and was interned—there are echoes of this in the early novel *Brot und Spiele* (Bread and Circuses, 1959); and then he worked for the British as an interpreter. He tells in 'Ich zum Beispiel' how he planned to falsify his own date of birth (a motif that recurs in *Der Mann im Strom*, The Man in the River, 1957), but saw that 'it was useless. My life had too many witnesses, and I was my own most severe prosecution witness.' Yet he refused for the time being to commit himself to 'any definite and unmistakable action' (Bez., p. 28). He studied for a time (his studies including philosophy, English and comparative literature) and was mildly involved with the black market, a theme taken up in *Lehmanns Erzählungen* (Lehmann's Tales, 1964). Then he worked for *Die Welt*, and the journalist appears frequently as a narrator-observer in his works. He lives now in Hamburg, and the literary local patriotism that marks much of Lenz's work has manifested itself in some short pieces, in the Hamburg portraits of *Leute von Hamburg*, and in the transplanted peasant world of Masuria in the tales set now in 'Bollerup', collected in *Der Geist der Mirabelle* (Plum Spirit, 1975).

'Ich zum Beispiel' ends with a brief statement of what Lenz sees as his literary themes: 'Fall, flight, pursuit or persecution, indifference, revolt, lives founded on shaky principles' (Bez., p. 31). Others might be added: motifs which preoccupy Lenz are those of duty (something else that he hints at in 'Ich zum Beispiel') and the *Grenzsituation*, the

13

borderline situation, requiring a decision that may well be a wrong one. He is concerned too, however, with perspective, with the impossibility of objective truth, something which he returns to time and again in his novels and short stories, and which becomes at once subject of the story in hand, and at the same time a specifically literary questioning. The notion of the witness and his responsibility recurs frequently in his work.

In an interview, originally for Hesse Radio in 1973, Lenz's fellow-writer Martin Gregor-Dellin asked Lenz about his insistence on the fact that one cannot write about other people without writing about oneself. Lenz responded that his writings were not purely self-justificatory, but rather were attempts to pose the question: how did this come about? Lenz shares with many of his contemporaries the theme of *Vergangenheitsbewältigung*, 'coming to terms with the (recent) past', and he shares with Heinrich Böll in particular the specific attitude that the past must not be forgotten in the brave new world of the economic miracle.

Lenz's chief literary models are—so he himself tells us—Hemingway, Faulkner, Dostoyevsky, and in Germany Borchert and Böll. The influence of the last-named is very clear, especially in the short stories—themes, titles, names of individual characters, sometimes stylistic devices: all these point to Böll. In an essay of 1968, 'Heinrich Bölls Personal' (Heinrich Böll's Characters, Bez., pp. 55–63), Lenz tells us that 'Böll's characters force irresistibly upon the reader a sense of contemporary fellowship . . . they make us become once again what we have, to be sure, all been for a long time, but what we refuse to admit, be it out of indifference or pusillanimity: that is, accessories to the facts' (Bez., p. 163). The term *Mitwisser*, here rendered as 'accessory' is a vital one, implying knowledge of, objective involvement in, and perhaps guilt for the past.

From Hemingway, whom he has described most specifically as his model, Lenz took first of all the figure of the loser, the figure trapped by some kind of force—by age, by history,

14

SIEGFRIED LENZ

by a 'borderline situation' in which there can be no right
answer. Indeed, the idea of a prison as such is frequent in
Lenz. Much of the style is Hemingway's, even when Lenz
made deliberate efforts to move away from the American's
influence, but Lenz is also reflective and mixes deliberate
masculinity with (sometimes contrived) aphorisms. Indeed,
his style as a novelist seems at times to recall Thomas Mann
as much as Hemingway, improbable as this may seem.

Camus, Sartre and Dostoyevsky may perhaps be grouped
together as providing the existential themes in Lenz's writing. Camus's influence can be one of simple scene-setting,
however, and Sartre's plays (which Lenz has acknowledged
as an influence) come more strongly to mind. In particular
Lenz is concerned with the idea of the hostage, placed in a
dilemma, frequently that of duty versus humanity, or of
divided loyalty. The motif is present in *Zeit der Schuldlosen*, in
Stadtgespräch (Topic of Conversation, translated as The Survivor, 1963) and in short stories. Sartre's plays *Morts sans
sépulture* and *Les mains sales* could be considered partial
models.

Lenz is an eclectic writer. The play *Das Gesicht* (The Face,
1964) recalls Chaplin's film *The Great Dictator* and—less
familiarly, perhaps, Miguel Asturias's *El señor Presidente*, a
work about which Lenz has written. One is frequently struck
by the familiarity of the themes, or indeed by the recognis-
ability of elements in the stories. Lenz appears to respond
from time to time to what might be thought of as a literary
Zeitgeist. His novel *Brot und Spiele*, for example, appeared at
about the same time as other sport-novels, including Alan
Sillitoe's novella *The Loneliness of the Long-Distance Runner*,
with which it has been compared. *Brot und Spiele* serves also to
illustrate an aspect of the genesis of Lenz's novels, and
indicates one of Lenz's major sources: his own writings. The
novel is in some ways an extended version of a short story
called Der Läufer (The Runner, written in 1951, included in
the collection *Jäger des Spotts* in 1959), although the ending of
the short story is distinctive and quite different, and the

15

character is not, of course, worked out to the same extent as in the longer work. Another portion of the novel links with the short story 'Der Amüsierdoktor' (Ph.D. in Entertainment, in *Das Feuerschiff*, 1960), although the shorter version takes a different course, while using the same character.

The incident is not isolated. Lenz has often reworked themes that began as 'Funkerzählungen' (semi-dramatised radio features) into short stories. Sometimes this has involved him in a shift of perspective, and the nature of observation is one of his main themes, as is the questioning of 'what is truth'.

Lenz often calls to mind experiments in the presentation of the problem of objectivity, such as Akira Kurosawa's film *Rashomon*, or literary manifestations, such as Faulkner. It is not only significant in terms of different objective perspectives that Lenz should rework themes: that there is a difference between the part played by the 'Amüsierdoktor' in the story and the novel is significant. In *Stadtgespräch*, Lenz uses the image of the delta, the river that takes any number of different channels, and this can be applied to his tales, and also to his reason for making them take different courses. In a recent short story, which will merit closer consideration, Lenz encapsulates the question of objectivity and developmental possibilities. In 'Phantasie' (Imagination, 1974, Ein.) three writers give different versions of how they imagine the circumstances that brought a man and a woman into the bar in which they are sitting. Lenz finally adopts the role of 'metanarrator', and has the man give a statement himself—thus we are offered as many possibilities as would be conceivably possible within a limited fictionality.

Three works may be looked at more closely in the attempt to evaluate Lenz's role as a writer: first, a commentary he wrote in collaboration with Dieter Seelmann on a volume of aerial photographs, *Flug über Land und Meer* (Flight over Land and Sea, 1967); secondly, the portraits in *Leute von Hamburg*; and finally the story 'Phantasie' of 1974.

At the beginning of the book of photographs, the problem is posed of whether it is even necessary to comment on photographs:

> Are they not definite and finalised? With every book we read, our imagination has to play a part. Does this apply with photos, too? . . . Is it possible for a photograph to provide us with an . . . optical adventure? If two people read the same book, the suspicion can be aroused that there are two different books involved. Will two observers of the same photograph experience the same effect?

And Lenz goes on to say how the commentary is an attempt on the part of the commentators—both of them—not to describe the pictures, but to place themselves in a relationship to them, 'to clarify the feelings, experiences and moods that the pictures called up in us'.[4] Everyone, say Lenz and Seelmann, is familiar with a map of his own town, but the impression that he has of the area itself is subjective. The attraction of the aerial photograph is the novelty of perspective, but the whole, however subjective the presentation, is still essentially documentary. Hamburg is seen from a new perspective, and it is interpreted through the conversation of the involved writers. But it is still Hamburg, and the photographs are there beside the text, taken by the *Deutsche Luftbild KG* (the German Aerial Photography Co. Ltd.), whose faceless official title is entirely appropriate.

Leute von Hamburg is an individual work of some sixty pages. In the ten years since it first appeared, it has sold some fifty thousand copies. The starting point of the work is of interest here, however, or what might be called the conceit on which the book is based. The aim is to establish the people of Hamburg, a task which Lenz sees as one which requires a special approach:

> In order to put your finger on the people of Hamburg, to become enthusiastic or put off by them, you need a special technique, you need a well-equipped eye, and a good supply of spare hours. The best thing is to take a rum-glass, one of the old-fashioned cut-

glass goblets with a long stem, and then ensconce yourself in the window-seat of a bar—or, if by some strange chance the sun happens to be shining, you can make it the veranda—and then after the necessary preparations the search can begin. Raise your glass across the path of the passers-by, and it behaves like a sympathetic lens, gathers them up and captures them. (LvH., p. 6 f.)

Different people come into view in this fashion, and Lenz speculates on them, having invented and then, as it were, captured them in a slightly distorted way in the glass. A girl is typified neatly and effectively:

You can see at a glance that the girl sets great store by the appropriate use of the word 'no' in all of the three languages at her command. A true daughter of the Hanseatic cities, she was born on the ferry between London and Hamburg, didn't need to learn English, only French and Spanish, and with the aid of these three languages she assists in the importing of fats and skins. (LvH., p. 8)

A mixture, therefore, of invention on the personal level, and general plausibility. Thus, too, the rest of the portraits, with sips of rum in between: a young businessman, a schoolboy with business tendencies, running a kind of proto-insurance-agency at school, and then a housewife. Heine is invoked at the beginning of the book, and comes to mind again here:

Perhaps she is Hammonia herself, the bourgeois goddess with the shopping bag . . . The goddess, with the air of a haddock and the shopping bag, reckons everything up in small change: in that way, all facets of life become visible and controllable. Italy, a country she once visited, will always be a bit suspect because the banknotes have such ridiculously high numbers on them. (LvH., p. 27)

By the time we reach the policeman, the rum is taking its effect—Lenz tells us that this is necessary, we are to half close one eye, or to incline the glass, so as to achieve a *deliberate* distortion. Nor is he incapable of playing with us,

18

once the conceit has been established, making us guess at the identity of the next character in the glass (a lady journalist, as it happens). In a way, the characters are a little predictable—the prostitute is there (honest, pretty well bourgeois herself, saving up her money), the dock-worker, the occasional eccentric. The whole is well done but not overdone. The conceit of the rum-glass is maintained and developed as a necessary distortion, but a distortion that will *lead* to reality, almost an emblem of the writer's craft:

> Drink, keep drinking, the rum-glass gets more talkative that way, captures and invents the people of Hamburg, people you wouldn't come across unarmed. Believe every second word the glass tells you and every third word of your own. (LvH., p. 68)

The last character (the glass and the rum seem to make the character into three) is a schoolmistress—a fairly frequent figure in Lenz's work. Through her Lenz leaves his series of vignettes in a sense of irony:

> She herself doesn't believe that man can be saved through his imagination, any more than through music or painting. She maintains a kind of wan hope in mathematics alone. (LvH., p. 69)

How sincerely she believes this, though, is left open, and she becomes in any case through the rum-glass *three* people.

The work is comparable with Lenz's story 'Phantasie'. Three writers at a convention meet in a bar, and notice a man and a slightly older woman. Lenz provides us with some other props—a matchbox and a feather in the woman's handbag. Then he lets the three writers exercise their own imaginations on the background, thus giving us three tales, three possibilities and three perspectives. Critics of the story have pointed out that all three are Lenz.[5] The first constructor of an imaginary life presents a realistic picture: the woman is the (married) lover of the man, forced to make an end, as her husband is being transferred abroad, but at the last moment it appears as if they will be exposed. The second

19

story—which is told by the first-person narrator of the whole piece—sees the couple as brother and sister; they have just seen their father, whom they have for years supposed dead, and have pursued and confronted him. He has denied this identity, although it seems true, but has told them to return later. They are waiting.

The reaction of the others to this story, told, it must be recalled in the first-person voice of the framework, is also interesting:

'Typical, just typical of you, old man. Everything left in the air at the end, because you think it isn't proper to have a conclusion'. (Ein., p. 295)

The third story is told by the writer, who is seen in the story as the one with the greatest reputation. His tale is pure fantasy—we recall the title, which in German means fantasy or imagination. The woman in his version is in possession of a feather which causes stone to melt away, permitting her to see the secrets behind ostensibly solid bourgeois walls. Eventually she tries to get rid of the feather, and at the end of the third narrative Lenz fuses the inner story into the framework:

She must get rid of it once and for all. One match is all that is needed.

Dieter Klimke was silent, and Gregor and I looked across to the pin-ball machines. The woman was just lighting a match, she dipped the feather into the flame and the light greyness bent into a sharp flame, spluttered a little, and became ash. (Ein., p. 308)

The central narrator is then made by the two other writers to approach the man in the bar, who turns out to have no connection with the woman at all. The whole is a conscious literary exercise. The three narratives are possible and realistic in the first case, more far-fetched but inconclusive in the second, and pure imagination in the third. Yet none is true, any more than the situation itself. As a whole, the story typifies Lenz's self-conscious approach to his writing, questioning the rôle and indeed the capability of the observer.

The styles are all his, however, and short stories can be found in Lenz's work which approximate to all these modes.

Lenz takes care with the person of the narrator, aiming in some cases to give an objectivity to the story, in others to suggest involvement, although sometimes the first-person narrator can seem superfluous. The charge has been laid at Lenz's door, however, that he is simply not involved enough. For a while he was active in support of the SPD, and published papers defending their policy regarding the Eastern Bloc in 1971. But this has played only a small part in his work, and some critics have taken him to task for this.[6] The criticism of his lack of political activism seems misplaced: Lenz aims his work beyond the sphere of the political, and to demand from him some kind of socialist pamphleteering is to miss the point of his novels and stories. Lenz has, however, discussed in an interview with the then Federal President Gustav Heinemann in 1973 the question 'What can the writer do towards peace', and has made enlightening comments on his deliberately non-engaged political standpoint, as well as on the problems of engagement.[7]

German writers since the war have suffered, in fact, from direct political involvement, and perhaps they are more vulnerable to criticism for errors than the politicians themselves; Böll's attitude to the early stages of the Baader-Meinhoff affair illustrates this. Lenz's rôle seems conceived as that of one with a social conscience. That *Der Spielverderber* (The Spoilsport, 1965) is the title story of a collection is not without significance. The central (narrator) figure is a spoilsport because he *remembers* things that others want to forget.

On the other hand Lenz, unlike Böll, is not theologically committed, although it is tempting to see patterns of guilt in his work which can be explained in terms of theological or doctrinal models. There are also biblical echoes in his work but these, surely, are part of the cultural heritage of Western writers.

Marcel Reich-Ranicki first dubbed Lenz 'der gelassene

21

Mitwisser', a term noted above as difficult to translate, but implying one who has come to terms with the fact that he is necessarily involved with the horrors of a horrible century.[8] *Mitwissen* might be rendered as *conscience*, however, and this seems to sum up Lenz's aim: that of conscience. In the concluding remarks of an interview between Reich-Ranicki and Lenz in 1969, Lenz referred to his then current literary project in a manner that typifies his artistic aim:

> Stories—stories that will certainly not be able to decide anything, but which might throw a small light on the nature of reality. (Bez., p. 215)

A few points may be made, finally, about Lenz's style. As Walther Killy has pointed out, it is unfair to continue to tax Lenz with the infelicities of the early writings.[9] There were infelicities, however. These included a tendency to employ in the manner of a *leitmotiv* points that apparently have the weight of symbolic use, but which, on close examination, simply do not bear that weight, and contribute little to the work. The early novels in particular show this and other faults of style: indulgent, pointless, overblown and sometimes erroneous nature description is a feature of *Duell mit dem Schatten* (Duel with the Shadow, 1953), but Lenz has, after all, not allowed a reprint of this work. A more lasting, if less unfortunate feature, is a seeking after aphorisms, which can all too easily become platitudes. Examples from *Duell mit dem Schatten* are easy to provide ('Even eating is an adventure,' Duell, p. 191), but even a novel like *Stadtgespräch* also suffers; there is a tonal similarity between the overtly portentous: 'Only in the recognition of a borderline do we come to assign a value to ourselves' (Stg., p. 99) and the line quoted from *Duell mit dem Schatten*.

In the Suleyken tales, on the other hand, this sort of philosophy is used as a comic device. Lenz's fault, then, is perhaps a lack of self-irony, even a failure to develop the comic lines of thought. He shies away from the complete *reductio ad absurdum* even in the satires, and when he does go the whole way (as in a scene in a hat factory in one of the stories where a museum of the 'history of the hat' contains St. Peter's yarmulke, in a burglar-proof case) the only impression is that Heinrich Böll has made a brief and not entirely appropriate guest appearance.

A more general critical point made about Lenz is the question of validity of material in respect of the genre chosen. *Deutschstunde* has been criticised for a length which is not merited by its subject-matter, *Das Vorbild* for being a pastiche, rather than a coherent novel. Lenz does indeed tend to blur the genre, but some of his works beggar generic distinction in any case. Thematic categorisations are equally difficult: Lenz is, it is true, preoccupied with themes such as duty, and responsibility within or outside a collective ideal. But he is also eminently capable of showing the lighter side of men and manners, observing humanity without reference to a real or transferred sense of original sin. The Suleyken tales must not be under-estimated.

In this study, we have of necessity to concentrate upon the major collected works—the five early novels and the two later ones; on Suleyken, Bollerup and the black market, on the satirical and the serious short stories in the four major collections, on the published radio plays (there are several unpublished radio plays). The position is, even so, that of an *embarras de richesse* rather than any paucity imposed on the critic by the age of the writer.

2

THE FATAL NOOSE: FOUR EARLY NOVELS

The unifying factor in Lenz's four early novels is the inevitability of failure: all are studies of human situations in which a single central figure is faced with a borderline that he cannot cross, although he tries. In the first story, *Es waren Habichte in der Luft*, a character refers to a story by Ambrose Bierce (who is not named), which may stand as an extended metaphor for much of Lenz's work. Bierce's story, published in 1892, is called *An Occurrence at Owl Creek Bridge*[10] and concerns a soldier during the American civil war who is about to be hanged:

> He stares at his arch-enemy, the rope, and sees with delight that the rope is very thin, and doesn't look as if it will take the weight of a man, but will break. The noose is put around his neck and tightened. There is a jolt and the poor man falls. There is a huge jerk, and the rope seems to break, he falls and falls, hits the water, surfaces again to get air, and the bullets are hitting all around him, so he dives under again and is carried along by the current for a good way, he gets to the bank, climbs out, runs, falls, gets a grip again, and always the bullets. At last he reaches the woods, and falls exhausted under a tree. But before he can fall asleep a wild cry wakes him. He jumps up, opens his eyes and sees that that thin rope took his weight very well, that he is dangling from the bridge, and the scream he heard must have come from the bridge . . . That must be a surprise. (Hab., 110 f.)

This is the key to the early novels: the rope appears to be thin, but it holds. Escape is a delusion, and we recall all the images of fate—the net, the pursuing furies, the illusion of an ability to mould one's own fate that is the basis of tragedy.

Es waren Habichte in der Luft was Lenz's first published

major work, and was accepted with enthusiasm most notably in a widely reiterated review in the *Frankfurter Allgemeine Zeitung* by Karl Korn.[11] The story is set in Karelia just after the First World War, after the new Russian régime has taken over. Teachers are suspect to the new government, and one has escaped the net of the new régime. The dangers facing the teacher are stated in the story:

> People who educate young people take themselves as exemplary . . . I mean, a single man can teach fifty others to think like him. (Hab., p. 84)

This is here put ironically, in the light of the régime in question, but the theme is also there in Lenz's most recent novel, over twenty years later.

One teacher has escaped—Stenka—and is trying to get across the border to safety. He is given work by Leo, a huge nurseryman, and shares a room with Erkki, who has been a pupil of his in the past. They do not give him away, but set against Stenka is a representation of evil in the form of a small and logical activist, Aati, referred to as 'der Kleine' (the little man) throughout. Stenka is tested against a limit, and there is an actual border involved for him to cross. In symbolic terms, Stenka uses this to establish what he is. The results are fatal. On the run, he accidentally witnesses a murder, is linked with it himself, and at the end is forced to flee through the woods—and through the stream, with strong echoes of the Bierce story—to the border. He is joined at the end by Erkki, also in flight:

> Youth is generally faster than age, on the racetrack of decision, faster on the level ground, faster. (Hab., p. 166)

Stenka is killed by a guard; Erkki is wounded, but makes it. The net, which was here from the beginning, has drawn itself round Stenka. Over the work too is the dominant symbol of the hawks—a natural image for the furies, watching and waiting, but not interested in the men as individuals.

The novel is not concerned only with Stenka. There is a

sub-story, that of Petruchka, a simple man whose wife has deceived him with his brother whilst he was in the army. Maddened, he takes an axe and wanders through the woods always searching for his brother. The daughter, Manja, works for the régime, is loved by Erkki, and is eventually killed by Petruchka while Stenka looks on. The whole is a parallel to the futility of Stenka's attempt to organise his own fate, and the interweaving of the stories is not unskilful. But Petruchka does not fit—the effect is of a character from a novel of Dostoyevsky, a *sanctas simplicitas* who has a purpose in life, but who is nevertheless mad—a man who abrogates to *himself* the rôle of the furies, and fails.

The style of the work is tense, and the action moves on well without the philosophical passages that characterise some of the later writings. The central story-line is strong and simple, and only the setting of the work is deliberately imprecise. We are clearly in Finnish Karelia, but what is never made clear is which border the central figure is trying to escape across. Nor does this matter. It has been pointed out[12] that the novel is from the time of the Cold War, and that it can be made into an East/West escape. This is irrelevant, and would in any case tie the work down to an historical limitation.

The symbolism of the work is clear, even sometimes over-done, although the hawks are by and large effective, and nature plays a considerable part in the story. Lenz has been criticised for an extension of the pathetic fallacy throughout this work and in others too, and to an extent the criticism is justified. Two examples may suffice, both towards the end of the work: first, 'A pear-tree groaned in its sleep,' (Hab., p. 154) and later still:

> The moon looked down on him with an I-told-you-so expression, and pulled a couple of clouds over itself to keep warm. (Hab., p. 160)

Not all of the nature imagery is like this, however. The water, and nature in general, are lasting. They contain an ancient story that men do not understand. Indeed, at the close, nature is personified as being beneficial. Erkki is wounded in flight, and falls when he is across the border:

> No one saw him, no one disturbed him when, after a while, he raised his head and crept slowly into the green, Spring-dull silence; the leaves whispered on, the friendly sky stretched out its blue breast and the sun, that glowing nurse, dried the blood. (Hab., p. 167)

And the novel ends with this optimistic, romantic faith in nature. Erkki has, however, been Stenka's pupil, made in his image, and his survival is positive in its implied continuity. The Bierce story dominates, and the true theme is that of guilt. As Hans Wagener has pointed out, Aati even links guilt with a rope around the neck:

> Everyone is born in the one-way street of guilt. In front of the only way out—into life—there is a huge mousetrap. (Hab., p. 152)

Aati abandons the subject, since it would be (as Wagener points out) politically suspect to develop it. But even if socialist realism has eradicated original sin, it is still there. The noose of guilt is the noose in Bierce's story, and age and weakness are just the outward manifestations of it.

Duell mit dem Schatten (Duel with the Shadow) which appeared in 1953 is the only one of Lenz's early novels not to have been reprinted, and although the initial reception was not unfavourable, recent criticism has supported this decision. Stylistically, this can be endorsed without reservation, but the novel is not devoid of interest.

The scene shifts from the northern setting of *Habichte* to an even more hostile environment, the Libyan desert. A German colonel has come there, in 1952, although physically very frail, to revisit with his daughter the wartime battlefields. To his daughter, Biggi, the colonel claims to be looking for traces of his friend Mackenbrandt, whom he was forced to leave during a battle. Biggi is separated from her father by a sandstorm, and she is saved by two Englishmen. The colonel falls into a disused shaft, where he engages in a

27

delirious conversation with two rats. He is brought out, presumed dead, by two men whose job it is to remove the many skeletons still left seven years after the war, and thrown on to a heap of skeletons on a lorry. He revives, and, trying to find his daughter, comes to the encampment of the English-men. A conflict which develops between the colonel and the one Englishman still in the camp is symptomatic of a general conflict between age and youth, and the daughter eventually associates herself with the Englishmen. It emerges that the colonel in fact had betrayed Mackenbrandt, leaving him to die while he escaped wearing his uniform. This precaution was to avoid recognition and blame for having caused the death of an airman in an incident during the war in which the colonel had apparently threatened the airman, who died, presumably of a sudden heart-attack. This incident is the pivot of the story, at the centre of the complex pattern of guilt. It is recounted in Mackenbrandt's diary, which Biggi finds amongst the colonel's belongings, and there the colonel is directly blamed for the death of the airman. Alaric, one of the two Englishmen, proves to be the soldier who had taken the colonel prisoner, and eventually the Englishmen take Biggi back out of the desert to the town. The colonel will not travel with them, attempts to walk, and collapses. His body is eventually found by the two skeleton-collectors, who ex-press satisfaction that he is now really dead: 'I knew this was where he belonged. He was just a bit late, that's all.' (Duell, p. 296). Two other events require mention. Near the camp of the Englishmen is a hermit, who has retreated to Libya in flight from the world. He realises the futility of his flight and returns with them and Biggi to civilisation. At another point, a group of tribesmen appear, engage the Englishmen in philosophical conversation, then leave, having robbed them of small items.

The style is frequently clumsy and W. J. Schwarz has drawn attention to a variety of stylistic infelicities in a devas-tating florilegium[13] from which one example may be trans-lated here:

Horace threw him an imploring glance; the glance reached its mark, bounced off and landed in the gravel. (Duell, p. 127)

For the English-speaker, the conversation in would-be English in Chapter 3 will provide evidence of a sometimes slipshod approach.

Much criticism has been levelled at the coincidences of the plot, and the ceremonious language of the colonel also places too great a strain on the credibility of the reader. This criticism is justified to an extent, but the work can be interpreted (whatever Lenz's intentions may have been) as allegory rather than realism. The Libyan desert is little more than an empty stage on which he can place his deliberately limited cast of characters, like figures in a medieval morality. At times the anonymity of Expressionist *dramatis personae* is recalled—*the* colonel—at others, the morality play proper. The bone-collectors are called Senger (= 'ravager'?) and Holebein ('bone-fetcher'), but perhaps with overtones of Holbein and the woodcuts of the *Danse macabre*. They *are* death. Their work underlines that of the leveller—the skeletons, usually unidentifiable, are all lumped together. The two Englishmen represent youthful vigour, as does Biggi. The hermit and the tribesmen have no character as such; not even well-motivated into the story, they embody philosophies for structural or general intellectual, and not human reasons.

The central character is the colonel, and his unreal and elevated speech sets him apart. For Biggi, he feels envy and even a kind of incestuous lust, but he is separate from her, and this is underlined by her association with the two Englishmen, younger, former enemies, and even different in rank. Insofar as they are drawn as individual characters, Lenz does stretch the credibility in, for example, the comments of Alaric on Prussian melancholy, in a passage which he borrows, incidentally, from Eric Williams's *The Wooden Horse*, narrating the escape from a POW camp by a secret tunnel. We may also ignore the improbable names of Horace

29

and Alaric, though presumably some Barbarian-Rome conflict might be implied, and the brothers are indeed different. But they are linked in their assertion of life—they are of the present:

> We came to visit this damned past of ours . . . but we didn't come to bask in old memories. You can't do anything with memories. The past—cold soup, worthless . . . what we are looking for here is our present. (Duell, p. 74)

The colonel is unable to cope with the present. He loses in a battle of nerves in which he points a gun at one of the Englishmen, and he loses his dominance over his daughter at the close, once she discovers the true relationship with Mackenbrandt.

The duel with the shadow is set up by the colonel, and is to be seen from his point of view, whether we take the shadow to mean the dark side of his own character, or his past as such. The standpoints of the Englishmen, while optimistic, still express a knowledge of existential guilt. Horace, in a comment that calls to mind Alfred Andersch's novel *Die Kirschen der Freiheit*,[14] states that 'In wartime the only chance a soldier has of doing right is to avoid doing wrong.' (Duell, p. 189). The colonel, however, is aware of personal guilt, and has come to Libya to settle his account with the past. This is not simply the German 'overcoming of the past', but is extended by the colonel into a broader philosophy:

> Accounting for one's actions means to settle up, it is a kind of self-defence . . . the desire to go back to a clean slate. Accounting for one's actions is to be tried by the present. I am prepared for the judgement. (Duell, p. 32)

Where the Englishmen voice the existentialist necessity of a continual coming to terms with the present, the colonel seems to see a determinism of guilt and punishment. His inevitable death is clearer than Stenka's inevitable failure to cross the border. His death is already entered in some metaphysical balance sheet. In the scene of delirium with the rats the colonel discusses inevitability, and the fact that the rats have been waiting for him. But he states very clearly:

> Creation has its own book-keeper; all ages are divided up, debit and credit. The card-index of existence is crammed full. (Duell, p. 20)

The death atones—like the scapegoat in the desert as well as personal punishment—on the one hand for the accidental death of the airman, on the other for the treachery against Mackenbrandt, but the precise nature of guilt remains unclear nevertheless. The airman was not the colonel's fault, and Mackenbrandt could not have survived in any case.

The hermit and the tribesmen—Tibbus—are merely functional. The former is a foil for the colonel only, and is indeed rescued from a cave by the Englishmen just as the colonel is (ambiguously) rescued by Senger and Holebein. The hermit has chosen to retreat from the world, fleeing from life to the desert (and in this the debt to Andersch is patent). He is brought back to life and taken back to civilisation. The colonel came back to the desert again to face up to things and dies in expiation of the past. In an interesting passage, the hermit comments that one can be dead without showing the physical signs, and the ambiguity of death is a dominant motif throughout.

The Tibbus too are functional and ambiguous. They seem to be the princes of the desert, and discuss their eternal pursuit of truth across the endless sands. Asked why they travel, they say:

> So that truth is constantly in flight, so that she stays young and elusive and swift, and doesn't become slack and indifferent. (Duell, p. 153)

This is the essence of the conflict. The younger people in the story, the existentialists, pursue truth just as Camus's Sisyphus continues to push the stone, heroically in spite of everything. The colonel pursues truth too, and finds it, although he has pursued a zigzag path, avoiding the marked

31

roads (these are further repeated motifs). He pays a belated account with truth, and the last truth is spoken by death.

Der Mann im Strom (The Man in the River, The Diver) appeared in 1957, and is in many ways one of Lenz's most completely successful pieces, avoiding as it does the stylistic excesses of *Duell mit dem Schatten*, and presenting a convincing story with a linear clarity that is not always present in *Deutschstunde*. The work links with the two first novels, in that it offers a study of a man facing old age in a society in which youth and health are at a premium. It is a social study too, of a man ageing in society, not in some outlying area, and is one of the few of Lenz's works to place a social problem in the foreground. The book was filmed in 1958, and this is indicative on the superficial level of the power of the story-telling.

Hinrichs is a diver, though to use this as a title would be to rob the work of an implicit symbol, that of the fast-flowing current of life, an image familiar enough to be accepted generally. He has a grown-up daughter and a young son (the pattern prefigures *Deutschstunde* and several of the short stories) and he needs work. The scene is Hamburg after the war, and there is work for divers, salvaging wrecks. The job, however, is not an easy one, and at fifty, Hinrichs feels the physical strain considerably, but worse, he will not be able to find employment.

> They need people everywhere, they can't get enough men, but they all want younger ones . . . With an older man it isn't worth the risk, not worth the outlay. (Mann, p. 10)

Hinrichs decides to make himself younger. He does this not in a way that inspires pathos—and the notion of an old man attempting to make himself younger is a familiar enough literary motif—but in an entirely rational manner, by cutting out neatly the date of birth on his papers, a symbolic and patently futile attempt to change what time has written. In fact it cannot be done neatly: his son sees where the changes have been made, although he pretends not to.

Hinrichs himself is aware of the net of lies that he is

spinning around himself: the symbolic underlay of the tragic net, that the hero himself weaves, is here again, as it was in *Es waren Habichte in der Luft*. In the end, Hinrichs is caught out, and loses his job. But the social point remains: constant reiteration of a slogan 'BE GOOD TO YOUR NEIGHBOUR'[15] underlines the hypocrisy of a society which, though polite to him, ignores all his needs for mental and financial support, and even his acts of bravery, recognising only his crime, that of altering his papers. It is ironic that he has to be dismissed when he has in fact proved his usefulness. Age and reality catch up with him, and the form taken by the furies this time is a younger man, Manfred.

Manfred has been trained by Hinrichs as a diver, but the character of the younger man is quite different. Whilst Hinrichs—and indeed his friend, Kuddl—are essentially honest, men of straightforward action, Manfred is shiftless and unreliable. Manfred had taken up with Hinrich's daughter Lena, and she is pregnant by him. She in fact attempts suicide but is saved and befriended by Kuddl, a figure of dependability. Manfred engages in various underhand activities, they spend their money on the cinema, and sleep with the vagrants under the huge Bismarck-statue. The symbolism is fairly clear: the Iron Chancellor (a 'hopeless look on his face') is in the past. Beneath him are these vagrants and petty thieves, the new men, ignoring the past entirely. Manfred, characterised as 'very young', and pictured with his hands in his pockets, is cowardly—so much so that Hinrichs cannot even hit him when he catches him stealing. Nor, though, can Hinrichs take proceedings against him, because Manfred has worked out the real age of the older man. Hinrichs even has to organise his rescue, just as Kuddl rescues Lena after a suicide attempt. Eventually, Manfred's inexperience tells against him, and he is killed trying to remove scrap using the wrong equipment, but by then he is no longer necessary. Hinrichs' forgery has been detected. Ironically he has, because of his experience, been able to suggest a means of raising a wreck that has saved much trouble, but the fact of the forgery remains, and just as

Hinrichs had earlier been beaten up by the young layabouts, he has to accept this, his ultimate defeat, with resignation, still aware of the fact that the changing of the documents was wrong:

> I made a mistake, and that was getting old. You can only permit yourself this mistake when you have a firm place somewhere. But being old and wanting to make a fresh start, boss, if you want to do that, you might as well get on the scrap heap right away. I should have thought of that. I feel like the wreck we just raised. I put a patch on the side, I did a grand job on my age, and I floated to the top again. But I should have reckoned that a wreck has scrap value and that's all. But what is more important than the scrap price is that the wreck gets cleared out of the harbour, so that new ships have enough room. (Mann, p. 154 f.)

The speech is a powerful one, and while it comes close to sentimentality (as do some of the Lena or Kuddl episodes), Hinrichs' straightforwardness saves it. Lenz does not labour the tragedy of his situation, but he shows us at the end Hinrichs with his son—Timm is a responsibility, but also a support. There is potential sentimentality in this scene too, of course, but Lenz does not underline the nature of the relationship between father and son.

The novel puts over well the feel of the docks and of diving, giving us throughout confidence in the accuracy of the narrative. There is symbolism, including the basic symbolism pointed out by Hinrichs himself, and some of it is unclear (such as the African king encounter at one point) but a good part of the narrative is almost documentary:

> They took an old keel as a patch for hull of the big wreck, and fixed it with screws over the leakage gap, and proofed the joint with tow and sailcloth. And then they put in a dozen pumps to clear the water from the wreck, and while the pumps were in operation, a diver kept constant check on whether the patch and its support were holding. The diver had a bag with sawdust that he dragged along the joint, and when you could see the sawdust getting into the body of the wreck, you had to leak-proof the join again. (Mann, p. 147)

What remains, however, is the final comment on growing old: 'There is really nothing you can do' (p. 155). There are two problems here: the social problem of age and work, and the personal problem, for which the only answer is that, tragically, there is no answer.

Of the four early novels, the most attention has been paid to *Brot und Spiele* (Bread and Circuses), which appeared in 1959, and this for two reasons: first, that it is an extremely well-executed piece of work, and secondly, that it is representative of what has been acclaimed as a new genre, The *Sportroman*. Whether this generic sub-division has any real staying power is, however, highly questionable.[16]

Lenz has himself described the genesis of the novel, and makes the point that he was interested in the way an athlete can become an example. More specifically, he links the idea of a race (*Lauf*) with *Lebenslauf* (*curriculum vitae*, course of life). Lenz is interested not in the runner as such, but in the runner *in his last race*. The theme of failure, the inability to run away any more, is the real theme once again. The work is conceived, then, as a symbol, and it is built up—very skilfully—on that premise. Lenz gives us the plot:

> The hero of the book, Bert Buchner, is a runner, a long-distance runner whose time of greatness is behind him. Without hope of winning, put in as a last-minute substitute more out of habit than conviction, he has been entered for the European (10,000 m) championship, and as he goes round and round the red oval he lives again, round for round, the stations of his life . . . I wanted to depict the temptations and pressures that a 'hero' is subject to: equal to the intoxication level of victory is the fear of defeat that will one day inevitably come. The fatal error of this runner lies in the fact that he equates his rise as a sportsman with a rise in life as a man. He takes sport to be something absolute, and refuses to think about the future . . . Bert Buchner pulls away from a good many competitors, but he can't run away from himself . . .

One final passage is vital to our interpretation. Lenz came, in writing the novel, to understand his central figure (and the

35

narrator, a reporter and life-long associate of Buchner, makes a similar remark):

> And I think that I came to understand him far enough not to seek guilt—if such a question should be allowed to arise anyway—on one side only.[17]

Buchner *is* a hero, and it is not too far-fetched to link him with the hero-figure of early Germanic literature. Doomed to fail (we are told this from the start of the novel), he still struggles against the tightening noose of age and inevitable failure. But the novel operates on two levels. The race itself is the present of the novel, the work 'takes place' during this last race, in a stylistic *tour de force* of maintained interest. In that race, Buchner is indeed heroic in his effort, for here he is racing against himself. During the race, however, the stages of his life as a hero in the *popular* sense are recalled, and here he has been anything but heroic: he has been deceitful, egoistical and at best shiftless. This past life leads Wagener, for example, to comment that his actual fall just before the end of the race is entirely deserved,[18] but this is true only up to a point—that is, it has a certain crude justice about it. In a more general sense, it is not the poetic justice of his failure that is relevant but the inevitability that a 'last race' will come. The poetic justice comes at best in the fact that Buchner has no trade; like others of Lenz's figures he has never completed his studies. This is the poetic justice: his collapse in the race is pure fate. What Buchner fails to see is that the race of life must always be run against oneself. Lenz underlines this point with one of the many classical references in the work. An old trainer, Lunz, is seen to be working on a history of the Marathon run—originally the absolute in human endeavour, which led, with a foreshadowing of Buchner's last race, to the collapse and death of the runner—be it Thersippos, or Eukles, or Pheippides, or Buchner. This idea contrasts with the implicit symbolism of the title, recalling the Roman circus, and the prowess of the participants is dependent not upon some absolute, but on the unreliable thumbs up or down of the public.[19]

The story is narrated by a close associate of Buchner's, a journalist professionally interested in the race. He is convinced at the beginning that Buchner cannot win, and becomes caught up in the excitement when it looks as if he has a chance after all. We also see Buchner's career through his eyes.

Buchner and another friend—significantly named Viktor—had been conscripted at the end of the war, but had deserted, making a plan that neither would allow the other to be taken alive. Viktor is wounded on the run, and Bert Buchner has to kill him with a bayonet. This sets the tone for the story—Buchner is running away from himself thereafter, and running *after* Viktor, or victory. The pursuers—and given the classical symbolism it is appropriate here to recall the furies—are always there. Later he runs from a British POW camp, and the shots behind him pre-echo those of the starter's pistol.

He joins a small local sports club after the war, and meets with the old man, 'Turnvater' Lunz, whose death affects him considerably. But it also turns him against poverty and leads him to stress the material side of life. He joins the rich club (Viktoria), deserting the small club, and also Thea, his fiancée, taking up instead with the wife of Gallasch, the 'Amüsierdoktor', a public relations man.

It is worth considering the relationship of the short story of that same name with its rôle here. The outline is the same—Gallasch (not named in the story) has a futile job in both versions. In the story, however, he becomes ridiculous (and provides amusement in the wrong way) when he is nearly killed in a fish-chopping machine. Here, while futile, and while probably representative of the type of member of the Viktoria club, he is first a pathetic foil to Bert's relationship with his wife. In an episode at the house of Gallasch, the specialist in amusement, Bert loses heavily at cards to Gallasch, but it is obvious where the wife's sexual preferences lie. Gallasch is drunk, desperate for the affection of his wife, and

37

aware that he has lost it to Buchner (who does, however, show sympathy—something underlined by the narrator). They go together to the fish-processing plant, and there is a real accident in which Gallasch's hand is trapped in the machine—or is it an accident? The desperate deed brings his wife back to him—the tale of Scaevola's proof of his integrity comes to mind, and the episode with Gallasch contrasts with Buchner's life. Buchner, on the other hand is capable of deliberate wounding of a rival runner with his spikes, of scheming to remove a rival from the team, but not of risking pain to himself.

The change to the Viktoria club comes at the physical central point of the work and of the race, but the narrator reminds us that half of the distance is not the same as half the race, and the book has a motto citing the Japanese proverb: 'If you have to run a hundred miles, then take ninety as the halfway point', and the same idea is invoked here.

Bert is not entirely negative. He has a moment of sympathy even for Gallasch, and is fond of Lunz. The narrative of his life is interspersed with fishing trips with the narrator, and this serves as an absolute, a non-competitive counter to his running. But the idea of the net and the fish, as indicated, are familiar tragic symbols, and we are reminded that fish are caught or indeed chopped up.

Bert's fatal flaw is the gradual domination of the pursuit of material gain, although even this had its comprehensible beginnings.

> I hate poverty, there is nothing I hate as much. There is no guarantee that it is any better than being rich . . . I've had enough of poverty, it doesn't make anyone better or happier. I know what you are going to say, but you can save your breath: you didn't see old Lunz on the floor beside his bed, you didn't have to undress him and wash him. (Brot, p. 55)

The confusion of the ends and the means, and the sacrifice of things that *are* worthwhile to the illusory impermanence of the immediate end, are tragic. This is not a sport novel as such: the theme is life, and the fact that men are pursued by external forces that they do not have the wit to recognise as the furies, and everyone is a victim.

The themes of the earlier novels are here too in more specific form, of course: that of ageing (*Habichte, Der Mann im Strom*) and of the impossibility of escaping from the past (*Habichte, Duell, Mann im Strom*) are all there, but the extended symbolism of this work makes the meaning wider. Bert Buchner is, it is true, a star, quite different from other men, and capable rather of general significance as a symbol, than as a subject for empathy at any level.

There are, though, two important characters in the work: Buchner, of course, the flawed hero, who can be understood, pitied—and can arouse fear for himself (the classical reflections in the work facilitate an Aristotelean reading of the story); and the narrator, his colleague, who advises him as a friend, who sides with Thea when jilted, who observes, and who understands and perhaps eventually pardons all. The question has been raised of whether the narrator is not perhaps also guilty, that he needs Buchner as a theme for journalism.[20] The speculation is interesting. But what comes over more strongly once again is the concept of being a witness. Perhaps the guilt of the narrator stems from the very association with Buchner. This points on to the next novel, the theme of which is that all men are guilty, and that to be a witness is to share in the guilt of life. With *Brot und Spiele*, however, the comments at the very beginning of the race are pessimistic:

> The runners are off. Already the first bend. They have passed the door to the circle of hell; to the inner or the outer circle? (*Brot*, p. 9)

Lenz seems almost, in this classically-titled novel, to be playing Vergil to the reader's Dante, and showing us a hell where *all* who enter must abandon hope, not just Buchner, the man who has 'no hope of winning'. The fatal noose is around everybody's neck.

3

WHAT IS TRUTH?: *STADTGESPRÄCH* AND 'DAS FEUERSCHIFF'

The novel *Stadtgespräch* (Topic of Conversation, translated as
'The Survivor') appeared in 1963 (and before that in serial-
ised form), and it serves as a bridge between the four early
novels, with their theme of failure, and the problems of
individual and social responsibility explored in *Deutschstunde*
and *Das Vorbild*. It may be compared, too, with the story 'Das
Feuerschiff' (The Lightship), written in 1959-60 and published in the collection of short stories to which it gave the
title in 1960. 'Das Feuerschiff' may because of its size and
many of its stylistic features be seen as at least a novella.

The basic theme of both works is the choice of evils
imposed when hostages are taken for any purpose. That they
come to different conclusions—insofar as they come to conclusions at all—is probably inevitable. The increase in kid-
napping as a political weapon over the past few years has,
moreover, sharpened the sensitivity of the reader to the
problems inherent in this kind of theme, but an increased
awareness of the possibilities of such a situation has not made
the possibility of a general solution any more likely. Lenz
does, of course, treat the theme in his drama *Zeit der Schuldlosen*, and the 'experimental' situation set up there is echoed
in these works, too. There is some justification for treating
the stories not in the order of composition but in that of the
events told in them. *Stadtgespräch* is set—in spite of efforts to
make the time and place deliberately vague—in Norway
during the Second World War. 'Das Feuerschiff' is set after
the war, although there is still a link with it. Both works have
enjoyed a measure of success, indicated, for example, in the

fact that both have been widely translated (far more so than the other early novels and short stories) and that 'Das Feuerschiff' has been filmed.

Stadtgespräch is potentially a war-time suspense story. A Scandinavian country is under enemy occupation, and in the town at the centre of the story, an enclosed, small community, a resistance group is formed only after two years, under the leadership of Daniel, a one-time student who has broken off his studies. As the work opens, Daniel and some comrades, including the narrator, are lying in wait for an enemy general. The assassination attempt fails, and the group flees, with Daniel badly wounded.

In reprisal, forty-four of the town's leading men are arrested: the local judge, bank manager, pastor, even the doctor, who is the narrator's father, and who had known the enemy Commandant as a student, and the local policeman, who has incurred unpopularity amongst the townspeople because of his collaboration. Daniel must give himself up or the men will be executed.

Daniel wishes to give himself up. He is, however, no longer Daniel, but 'DANIEL', a sign scrawled on walls in token of the *idea* of resistance, and the partisans will not allow him to give himself up. A counter-attempt to kill the Commandant fails, events in the town itself lead to the betrayal of the resistance hideout in the mountains, and a move is forced. The Commandant refuses to give way even when a group of his own soldiers are taken counter-hostage. Daniel does not give himself up, the hostages are shot, and even the request that the men be buried by their own people is rejected.

Eventually, the occupation is ended, the Commandant kills himself, and the *status quo* is restored. At this point the 'discussion' begins, most of it hypothetical—'what would have happened if—but also blurring things that we have already been told from an eye-witness point of view. Daniel is accused, and when, after an attack by a man whose son was amongst those shot, he kills the man in self-defence, his arrest

41

provokes the comment: 'Now it's his turn. Now he'll pay for it.' (Stg., p. 190). But he escapes from the prison hospital and disappears, retreating to a place where, it is presumed, he can tell his own story.

The tale is told by a first-person narrator, not Daniel, but one of his followers. It is, moreover, an address *to* Daniel, a statement to the effect of 'this is the story as *I* remember it—you must tell it from your side.' Further, there is no suspense as to whether Daniel actually does give himself up. The work opens with a series of hypothetical questions:

> And if Daniel had given himself up? And if the whole town had supported him with one voice in not giving himself up? Would his story have finished then? (Stg., p. 5)

The narrative strategy of the novel is for the most part successful. Sometimes it is stretched, as indeed it is in *Deutschstunde*, where the narrator has to be made to be present to overhear a conversation. Here, there is a vital conversation between two of the hostages, and the narrator has to be placed in a position to eavesdrop and report. Sometimes, though, the omniscient narrator intrudes willy-nilly: this is clear in the description of the death of the hostages. The resistance fighters hear the shooting and imagine what is happening, and the narrator imagines it in great detail, but he does so through Daniel:

> Daniel . . . said something, but I didn't catch it. Did he hear something? Did you hear more than we did? Were you there ahead of us in your imagination? Did your mind draw a picture of the event for which there were no eye-witnesses? No, no eye-witnesses for this part of the story, this chapter was played out without any audience, who could pass on the details; they took the event from us, and left us the consequences.
>
> But the consequences suffice, they are always enough for a patient eye, even if the looking blinds us. And I saw it all, Daniel. I went with them, while you were lying there beside me, your mouth open, your hands pressed over your ears. (Stg., p. 131)

And the mind's eye of the narrator tells Daniel in great detail,

42

adding even a soldier who refused to join the firing squad and was shot himself. The vividness of this incident, where the imagination overtly takes over, makes more real the supposedly involved narrative of the rest. The problem of narrative reality becomes more acute if we compare the shooting with the hurried flight of the resistance fighters from their camp, something which presumably did have witnesses:

> What happened up there in the camp when the sentry rushed into your tent and didn't need to say a word, just to point at the file of soldiers as they climbed nearer to make clear that a move was necessary? Tell that, Daniel, if you think it is worth telling. (Stg., p. 84)

The rôle of the narrator as a witness is made clear in one incident within the story: one of the fighters is selected to try to kill the Commandant, as an expiation of an earlier act against the spirit of the resistance. He is to be accompanied by the narrator, whose rôle is simply to observe:

> Christoph knew that he had to act alone, and that I was to be no more than a mirror, which would take disinterested cognisance of his actions and illuminate them. (Stg., p. 74)

His job is not to judge, any more than the rôle of the narrator (or the author?) is to judge the whole. The fairly obvious setting of the work in Norway makes the place and time of the action immediately apparent, although Lenz never makes it clear. One wonders why not.

Lenz builds upon the fundamental dichotomy between good and evil, a basic contrast between occupiers and occupied which is clear, and against which the more complex problems of how a single community responds may be set. To draw overtly on the historical opposition in Nazi-occupied Norway would seem to have been more appropriate.

The occupiers are portrayed negatively: Daniel began his resistance when a soldier shot down a boy, and the Commandant is a pragmatist without apparent regard for the lives of his hostages or his soldiers. One man's (or one

43

epoch's) partisan is another man's terrorist, and Lenz would presumably not want any confusion of loyalties to occur later. It is significant that Lenz's next novel—*Deutschstunde*—is in a deliberate historical setting. Here, incidentally, there is a distinction between the Commandant and the group of semi-invalid conscripts taken counter-hostage by the partisans.

Superficial tension, then, is precluded by the opening paragraph: we know Daniel has survived, as indeed has the narrator. The story again recalls the basic tenet of the heroic epic, which shows a human figure struggling against a destiny which is inevitable, and since it *is* inevitable, can be told from the beginning. *Stadtgespräch* reverses the fate of the medieval hero, however: it is Daniel's fate to survive, not to die. When a hero of the Germanic epic died in an inevitable struggle, he found glory, and was aware of this. Daniel's fate in surviving is to find accusations and whisperings against him—a *Stadtgespräch*, not an heroic poem.

The opening of the work does not preclude tension within the story, of course: the incidents that arise from the basic situation have an inner tension that contributes towards the readability of the work. These incidents sometimes take the story in unexpected directions, but all are related to the central theme of Daniel.

Daniel is doomed to failure from the beginning. The resistance started too late:

> Everyone knows that it came late, the town had been occupied for two years, we had come to terms, subjected ourselves, got used to it; we had discovered that it is possible to live without justice. (Stg., p. 41)

What Daniel demanded was a different attitude, and his transformation into the embodiment of resistance becomes clear in the more philosophical portions of the novel. The first of these is a conversation between Dr Lund, the narrator's father, and the pastor, both hostages, overheard by

the narrator as they discuss their fate.[21] Dr Lund is aware of
the nature of Daniel's predicament:

> He is less fortunate than we are, whatever he decides to do . . . I
> believe that he will be taking more upon himself if he doesn't give
> himself up; not only would he have our deaths to bear, but with
> his every future action he will have forty-four dead men watching
> him. (Stg., p. 80)

He goes on to express the view that the forty-four hostages
are indeed outweighed by the idea of resistance to a government that is wrong.

The pastor presents the counter-arguments. The first is
that Daniel was not empowered by the hostages to act as he
had done. This is readily countered. Daniel has implicitly
demanded the 'duty of presenting a united front' (Stg.,
p. 81). But the pastor's next argument carries more weight: 'I
shall go against any claim on Daniel's part that he has killed
in my name.' (Stg., p. 81). This is not because of any expressly Christian ethic, but because Daniel came too late:

> Yes, at the beginning I was waiting for a confrontation too. At the
> beginning everything called for us to pitch cruelty against
> cruelty, will against will. Daniel organised the resistance in this
> town when we were already thinking about forgiving our
> enemies. (Stg., p. 81)

Dr Lund, who is patently resigned on the personal level, who
has, he tells us, made use of the limitation to his life to
understand himself, has the last word. His answer contains
too the possibility that the book as a whole could become a
kind of paradigm in this kind of situation. Just as Dr Lund
has taken the event personally, so he at least can generalise
on the impossibility of generalisation:

> There is nothing, pastor, that could outweigh the lives of forty-four
> men: no idea, no principle, no general truth. And anyway, I don't
> believe in general truths; I only believe in the truth of the given
> moment, the truth of what I have to face, what forces me down . . .
> we have to thank Daniel for the fact that what happened at the

beginning stays in our minds . . . One man's resistance forces us to compare our own situation with his, and reminds us that a state of injustice is not a normal state. Through his pressure we are forced to test how far we can go. (Stg., p. 82)

Daniel's efforts, however tragic they might appear, are the imposers of the necessary moment of truth, the urge to make those involved state what is right and what is not. The pastor's notions of forgiveness might be sincere, but ultimately they are flabby. The irony is that the central figure here—Dr Lund—and the one who understands, has to die. The rest of the people in the town do not understand, or if they do, they do not remember when the state of injustice is passed.

Daniel himself is a passive figure, and the echo of the 'lions' den' is presumably intended. The forces are beyond his control and he becomes aware of his own impotence. Whilst awaiting the noise of the executions, he agrees that

everyone is in his own prison, and the worst prisons are those in which we are both prisoner and jailor in one person. (Stg., p. 123)

Daniel does not develop in the work, but the awareness of the passive nature of his own suffering constitutes an anagnorisis.

Dr Lund is not the only person aware of the fate of Daniel. The narrator is approached by Daniel's old teacher (who has played a rôle throughout) and is told:

Give him regards from his old teacher . . . and tell him nothing has changed, he has never disappointed me, we shall try to understand him. Perhaps we shall have to learn to understand him. (Stg., p. 155)

But it is just after this that the discussions begin:

That is still going on and hasn't quietened down, this yea, yea and nay, nay, regular as the seasons, that we all know like a children's rhyme. (Stg., p. 157)

Gespräch is the theme of the work, and these conversations about but after the events contrast with the fact that the

46

partisans rarely communicate in words. Phrases like 'he signalled that I should do something' occur too frequently to be ascribed just to the necessities of the plot. Daniel indeed *becomes* a sign. These signs, moreover, are never ambiguous. Only after the events are the realities distorted by 'conversation', and this comes to a head in the attitude to Daniel's arrest. People have made up their minds what the answer to the opening question—'What would have happened if . . .'—is, and have not understood that the very question is irrelevant. Daniel has to break out of his real prison at the end in order to be able to tell them as far as he can what happened. But the hypothetical is always irrelevant to historicity, and the narrator points this out too:

> Every history has its delta, with lots of branches and possibilities, and because our story is ramified and insoluble, we shall have to reiterate it constantly. (Stg., p. 71)

This passage, which has been quoted regularly, is perhaps the key to the work. *Geschichte* can mean 'history' or 'story', and here it means both, combined in the delta image (one which Heinrich Böll has used recently in the opening to his *Verlorene Ehre der Katharina Blum*). There is no single answer to the problems of responsibility raised here: there are only individual answers that may or may not combine in the face of a great evil, and these too may be forgotten when the evil is past.

Minor episodes reflect the major problem. At the beginning of the work, after the failed assassination of the general, the narrator is hidden in the house of the old teacher, whose son, incidentally, is one of the hostages, in spite of fears by the rest of the family that he will endanger them. This is the whole situation *in parvo*, but in this case there are no far-reaching consequences, but it points to a possible progression: one man, a resistance movement embodied in its leader, and ultimately a possible overthrow of the whole enemy régime.

Christoph is 'condemned' to try to kill the Commandant because he had put his personal interests before those of the

47

group. He undertakes this, although he dies in the failed attempt, as so many of the moves in the story fail. On the way, however, he sees that the hideout has been revealed to the soldiers, and he returns to warn the group before continuing. This is a private act of expiation parallel to his 'public' undertaking, and he has come to terms with the judgement passed upon him. This is another instance of the problem of establishing how to act for the greatest good, his ultimate self-subordination to the group being a parallel to Daniel's enforced hiding. The narrator comments:

> Think of that when you talk about Christoph, and think too that you have to take his side just as you have to take everyone's; it is more important to understand than to condemn. (Stg., p. 68)

More problematic is Ole Dagermann, the one figure in the town side to be developed, and the only person to undertake resistance on his own, even if these acts are entirely personal in their motivation. Interestingly too, his acts are superficially more successful than those of the organised resistance. He is the brother of Jutta Nielsen, wife of the local policeman. Although the policeman has himself been taken with the hostages, his wife becomes a scapegoat in view of his earlier co-operation with the occupying forces. The wrath of the mob is turned on her, and she and her child are beaten. Ole Dagermann's anger at this is directed in its turn at Daniel, however. When a little later, Jutta is refused milk for the child, his feelings are too much for him and he betrays the location of the camp. Yet he is aware, too, of the nature of collective guilt, and of the impossibility of avoiding some guilt if the occupation is accepted:

> They [the dairy-owners] are behaving exactly as if they were pure and spotless, they are all convinced that they could live for years under the occupation and get on with their work properly, without getting a bit of dirt on their hands. They don't do anything, say neither yes nor no, do neither that which is forbidden, nor what is required, they just play dead, like some insects do when you touch them with your foot. No milk for the child! (Stg., p. 63)

Dagermann acts entirely for himself, but in acting positively he indicates the complexity of the problem. He takes the initiative, though from the wrong motives, perhaps, ostensibly on the grounds that someone must do something. On the second occasion he acts against the occupation. When the hostages are dead, Dagermann makes the sole and futile gesture of reprisal, blowing up and sinking his own ferry.

The question arises, and is at once asked: what good has the sabotage done? It has provided satisfaction for Dagermann, but perhaps little else:

> 'Well,' said Holmsen, 'did it do any good?' 'At least he did something,' said the judge's brother. 'Indeed,' said Holmsen, 'he did something. I understand what you mean by that, and what the other people mean who think the same way. But what you don't know is what it means occasionally to refrain from doing something.' (Stg., p. 156)

Dagermann's act is understood and applauded, but it is again one of individual anger. Last time it was against Daniel, this time against the régime, but it was not part of a unified stand. An erratic act, even if it has popular support, is irrelevant in the long run. Holmsen, the old teacher, points out the importance of Daniel's refraining from action.

The work has implications for the single individual in an extreme situation, and it has links with the earlier novels. For Dr Lund, the fact that he is faced with death forces his awareness of existence. Indeed, the whole incident in the town is testing:

> A line ran through the town, a shadow-line, a line of decision. It was visible and palpable already, it concerned everyone. (Stg., p. 32)

Daniel forces the people of the town to stand on one side of the line or the other.

The second set of problems in the novel concerns historical objectivity, and added to this is the notion of overcoming the

49

past by remembering it. Lenz illustrates here the basic lesson of history; that men never learn lessons. It is not the forces of evil that are castigated, but those who forget afterwards the whole necessity of resistance to an evil force, but rather remember only the concrete losses of forty-four men and a ferry. Those lives must also be set against humanity, not against Daniel.

The problem of objectivity takes the novel beyond its chronological limits, into historiography itself. In a short time the sequence of events becomes distorted, and even Daniel hears from the prison guard at the end a version of one incident that contrasts with what has been told us by the narrator as an eye-witness. This brings about the ultimate paradox: the story has to be reiterated, in order to keep it fresh.

> Something that happens without witnesses hasn't happened, Daniel, so we have to take the risk of making ourselves witnesses, we have to force ourselves to rehearse the whole thing again, live through it, cross-examine it; then it will come to life again, and we shall be able to tell the story. You can be present in a variety of ways, what counts is how much you retain and repeat. (Stg., p. 132)

Stadtgespräch is not paradigmatic in any practical sense. In a passage which, in this novel, is unusual in its sententious-ness, we are told that:

> Past credit-marks don't let anybody off the responsibility for a present action. For us, all that counts is how we survive and the one thing that tests us daily: the present. (Stg., p. 50)

Recent experiences with terrorism have shown all too clearly that every case is different. In 'Das Feuerschiff', however, Lenz does seem to be setting up a political or at least an ethical paradigm. This time the forces of terrorism make an attack from outside on to the picture of order, and the black and the white are clear again from the beginning. The problem is not in determining who is the terrorist, but rather how one is to react to terrorism. More even than in *Zeit der Schuldlosen*, we are presented here with a test-tube situation, an experiment, an exploration.[22]

Freytag is captain of a lightship at anchor in a channel which has been dangerous because of the mines and wrecks left from the war. It is about to be withdrawn from service, however, and this is the last spell of duty. Freytag has on board with him not only his small crew, but also his son Fred, who despises him, for reasons which are not immediately clear, and which form the sub-plot of the work.

A small boat is spotted by the son and its crew rescued, but it turns out to contain an unlikely trio, two thugs and the sinister Dr Caspary, who have just committed a major robbery. They are armed, and have effectively taken the lightship hostage. Their threats of violence ensure that the police are not called, and Freytag, to avoid hurting any member of his crew, agrees to their demand that their boat be repaired. The crew, however, will not do this and eventually it is cut free. This forces a showdown: Caspary demands that the lightship be loosed from its moorings to take them to freedom. Here, however, Freytag stops. He faces the gun aimed at him and is wounded, but does not give way. By now the police have been alerted, however, and the remaining two criminals—one has been killed, as has one member of the crew—are taken prisoner. The order of the sea has been maintained.

The sub-plot is concerned with the attitude of Freytag towards violence. Until the ship itself is threatened, and thus the whole concept of order at sea, he gives in to the demands of the three terrorists rather than risk harm to his crew. His son demands action, and reveals that his distaste for his father stems from tales of an incident in which his father was involved when in command of a sea-going ship. The ship had been lying off a Greek island with a cargo of grain, forbidden by the shipping company to put in and unload, in spite of famine, until the price could be forced up. The father and two others were held when the grain was eventually unloaded, were tortured, and only two returned to the ship. Freytag had refused to risk the entire crew to return for one man. The son understands neither this nor the attitude Freytag adopts towards Caspary and his accomplices, and the point of 'Das Feuerschiff' is precisely to explain that attitude.

Freytag realises that individual heroics are unsatisfactory, and acts—heroically—only when the entire concept of order is threatened:

> I was never a hero, and I don't want to be a martyr, because both have always struck me as highly suspect; their death is too easy, they were still sure of themselves and their cause even in death—too sure, I think, and that is no solution. I've known men who died so that something could be settled: they didn't settle anything, they left it all behind them. Their death may have helped them, but nobody else. If you have no weapons and no power, you still have more possibilities, and I often think that behind the wish to face the guns at any price lies the worst sort of egotism. (Fs., p. 55)

This was what Dagermann in *Stadtgespräch* failed to realise, too.

'Das Feuerschiff' fits well into the mould of the nineteenth-century novella. There is a concentration of space, time and action, a limited cast, a 'remarkable incident' and a dominant symbol.[23] The symbol is that of the lightship, there all the time, lighting a path through the treacherous waters, embodying *Ordnung* (order). The phrase 'bounden duty' takes on a new meaning here, and Lenz develops the paradox that the ship is tied—a prisoner to duty. Yet freedom is, for the ship, illusory—to unmoor it would mean to destroy the order of things.

The parable-like nature of the story as a whole is underlined in the character of Caspary (whose name perhaps evokes Dr Caligari?). The seamen are real: Freytag has been at sea for many years, has learned much and has realised the rôle of order and fixedness; and if the rest of his crew have some memorable attributes, such as Gombert with the crow as a pet, they are none the less real. Caspary is not a caricature, although the thugs who accompany him are more or less so; they lack depth, and their attributes are physical. That they are two brothers give them an air that is faintly Tweedledum and Tweedledee, but the interest is in any case on Caspary, who is characterised (as Lenz so often does his sinister figures) with a gesture—here polishing a large ring—and with his dark glasses.

He is, of course, an allegorical figure: the force of evil itself. He has assumed the identity of his twin brother, a lawyer (another favourite theme of Lenz), and has also been a large-scale blackmailer. Lenz places him in opposition to, and in discussion with Freytag: the seductive force of evil is set against the principle of order. This is the experimental centre, the philosophical thesis of the work. For Caspary's activities as a blackmailer have a philosophical basis. As a lawyer he had realised that

> everybody, but everybody can stand accused. Rich, poor, widows and orphans. Take anyone you like, and I guarantee that I'll find out something about him that would get him two years according to law. And that isn't even being severe. The only thing that stops the world being turned into one big court is the fact that the judges have too much to do and also the fact that there isn't anyone who would accuse them. (Fs., p. 92)

True or not, this is the voice of the serpent of the temptation, but after the Fall. Original sin, or perhaps in a non-theological context 'original evil', does not demand cynical acceptance, it demands an imposed order. Caspary sneers at this: 'Order, Captain, is the triumph of a lack of imagination', (Fs., p. 29) 'Phantasie'—the imagination that Caspary is so proud of, but which is such a danger. Imagination is a dangerous thing after all, and we recall that another German word for imagination is 'Einbildung', which can also be a 'delusion of grandeur'.

Here as in so many of his works, Lenz is writing about guilt as a state of being. Paradise may be an ethical prison, but it is still Paradise, and the way to return to Paradise is to impose on oneself the prison of order. The lightship has to be tied, and this is the basis of the work. It is—sneers Caspary—'a born prisoner' (Fs., p. 29), as is Freytag. But

> if a ship goes down, then it is a single tragedy, and is part of the price that you have to pay when you follow the sea. But if a lightship leaves its post, the whole order of the sea is finished. (Fs., p. 29)

For this reason, when that seems possible, Freytag *does* act heroically. His last words in the story are addressed to his son: 'Everything in order?' (Fs., p. 103)—and it is. This applies to the ship and now to his relationship with his son, who now understands him.

Given the strong allegorical mould of the work, it must be stressed that the tale is again a gripping one—more so perhaps than *Stadtgespräch*. Here we have too the superficial showdown tension, a German *High Noon*, and a narrative where the philosophical interludes—the debate between Freytag and Caspary—are less obtrusive. Elements of real tension are built in: one of the two criminal brothers is killed, and Caspary is taken prisoner, but released. One of the crew is also killed. There is an attempt on the part of the criminals to suborn a member of the crew, and, towards the end, a storm blows a live mine towards the ship. Freytag utilises the weapons and skill of the criminal Eddie to fire on and detonate the mine, thereby saving ship and pirates, and the political implications are interesting: a man without weapons has saved a situation by using the weapons and the force of evil. The concepts of the greatest good and the end as justifying the means are invoked. The incidents must be taken as they come, but order must prevail over all else.

4

DEUTSCHSTUNDE

Deutschstunde (The German Lesson, 1968) has been Lenz's most successful novel to date. Translations and a widely-shown film version have made this work one of the best known examples of German fiction of the post-war era. Lenz stated in an interview that he did not anticipate such success in view of the novel's theme, a 'conflict between power and art presented through the example of a ban imposed on a painter in Germany.' (Bez., p. 207). But this simple formula does not explain the success of the work, nor does it reflect, fully, its thematic implications. It is an investigation of the German past and its relationship to the present as experienced and narrated by a young boy, Siggi Jepsen. Like so many of Lenz's works it is a story of failure, but a far more subtle and penetrating analysis of the reasons for failure than the earlier novels: it is the failure not only of the central character, but of a society. Although the past is viewed through the perspective of one rather exceptional child, and is geographically and socially limited, set in a small community on the German-Danish border, within it are presented the dominant traits of a society and elements of a national psyche. Whilst this microcosm of Germany may seem to omit the more familiar events of the German past—the excesses of violence and inhuman bestiality—it reveals social and mental attitudes upon which Nazi ideology was based and accepted.

Lenz has been criticised for the parochial nature of the work, which tends towards the *Heimatroman* (Regional Novel), a genre that enjoyed particular popularity during the Nazi period precisely because of its insistence on the virtues of the natural life and local patriotism. But Lenz does not use the restricted horizon of this form to preach such virtues, but rather to illustrate the dangers of parochialism and the blind prejudice that stems from a restricted view of the world. He has referred to the use of such restricted vistas as exemplary:

> The great becomes transparent in the small, in the distant tragedy our own tragedy is discovered, the world is extended through the exemplary investigation of a—comparatively—small region. (Bez., p. 91)

Investigation is a word that recurs in Lenz's theoretical writings; he considers the writer's craft one of investigation, and questioning. His task is 'not to solve the questions of existence, but to ask questions of existence.' (Bez., p. 224) The investigation and questioning are here conducted by the narrator, Siggi, on behalf of his author and his audience.

The theme is, however, not simply that of the past, but also its continuation into the present; it suggests that there is no break in the continuity, and that the collapse and restructuring of society was only a superficial process beneath which older mental attitudes persist.

The novel works on two chronological levels: a framework narrative, set in 1954, and an interpolated account of the past spanning the years 1943 to the fictional present. But, unlike the traditional use of the framework narrative, the novel constantly shifts from past to present. The past is presented in an episodic manner which, whilst having a linear progression, may appear disjointed and arbitrarily selective. Theodor Elm has seen within this a reinforcement of the theme of the inability of the narrator to come to terms with the past, since the asyndetic structure lacks any synthesising idea by which a coherent interpretation of the past can be given.[24] But this seems only partially true.

In the fictional framework, the narrator is in a corrective institution for juvenile delinquents. He has been placed in the reformatory after admitting the theft of a number of paintings. He undergoes a process of rehabilitation, preparation for re-integration into society, which may be seen as a symbolic representation of a process of re-education that the German people needed to undergo during the post-war years with the move from dictatorship to democracy. The suggestion is, however, that this process is only a superficial one.

The complacency with which the head of the institution and the majority of his staff face their educational function, and the very qualities which they attempt to inculcate in the juvenile inmates, are presented as precisely those features that dominated the apparently forgotten past. Thus the youths are set the task of writing an essay on 'The Pleasures of Duty', a project that Siggi is unable to tackle in the time allotted. The essay title is indicative of an unregenerate society which can still, unquestioningly, believe in such unqualified and therefore hollow moral forms. Having failed even to begin the prescribed task Siggi is punished by being placed in solitary confinement until he has made some effort to make up for the deficiency. His problem is not that he has nothing to say on the so-called pleasures of duty, but that the whole of his past life is brought to mind, as is the very reason for his having been placed in the institution.

Siggi begins his essay, which he then feels compelled to complete at length, despite being told on occasions that he has written sufficient to demonstrate a contrite attitude towards those in authority. The essay, written over a number of months, turns into a detailed account of his childhood in an attempt to investigate his own past and to find some explanation for it and his own criminal development. What begins as a punitive imposition turns into a self-imposed task, a duty to re-experience the past in an attempt to understand it and learn from it. For his teachers the subject is unproblematic and indeed educative, thus they fail to understand his obsessional involvement with his past life.

The head of the institution, Himpel, warns Siggi of the dangers of dredging up the past:

Memory, it can be a trap, a danger, the more so because time heals nothing, nothing at all. (D., p. 15)

At the end of his account of his own past Siggi reaches what appears to be the same conclusion:

Bordered by these people, surrounded by memories, saturated by the events of my home region, undermined by the experience that time heals nothing, nothing at all . . . Failure through Rugbüll? Perhaps one could term it thus. (D., p. 415)

But the similarity contains diametrically opposed attitudes. Himpel is confident of the possibility of education, of the reconstruction of society, and dismisses the past as the haunt of unpleasant memories that have no relevance to contemporary life. Siggi, in contrast, realises that the past is in fact ever-present, not simply as memory, but as an unbroken historical continuum:

I see that nothing comes to an end, nothing stops, I'd like to tell the whole story again, differently, as a punishment. (D., p. 243)

For Siggi, everyone has the moral duty continually to investigate his own past, regardless of whether it has had such disastrous consequences as in his own life. For Siggi this permanent process of comparing past and present and re-objectivising the past is the only true education and corrective process; it is the punishment that each must regard as one's moral commitment to life. Elm's remark that the re-experienced past is presented by Siggi without any commitment and therefore without any synthesising idea is not entirely true because Siggi is conscious that he is in part a creation of the past and investigates it under this aspect: 'I have to confirm the pleasures of duty, trace its effects, which culminate in me' (D., p. 17). The scenes from the past must of necessity be selective. They are, however, not 'arbitrarily selective' (D., p. 14) as Siggi himself confirms, but are intended as a completely objective record. Siggi approaches this not without preconceived ideas, but these are in the form of a negative commitment, a conviction that judgement fixes facts in a manner that may simply be prejudice:

> I am not writing about just any region, but about my own region, I am not searching out just anyone's tragedy but my own tragedy, in fact, I am not just telling any story, because any such random story does not commit one to anything. (D., p. 179)

Siggi here uses the word 'verpflichten' (to commit, to impose a commitment), which is linked with the word 'Pflicht' (duty), the problem that stands at the centre of his account of his own life. The use of the word is not incidental. Siggi's conviction is that, unlike the fixed idea of duty, his own duty is to distance himself from events, suspend any final judgement, since one would thereby offend against the nature of the world, which does not exist as the reliable reality which the judgement we place upon it attempts to make it. Siggi does pass judgement on figures from his past, but only in so far as they either do not conform to this form of uncommitted conviction, or betray a belief in it.

This form of objective record accords with Lenz's theoretical views on the nature of literary reality, as compared to the scientific truths applicable to reality. Lenz expresses this in the following way in the essay 'Difficulties in Writing the Truth':

> Although my life is verifiable, enclosed and even determined by such factual truths, I do not believe that the whole truth is contained in their sum: it seems the whole truth is something that exists alongside these numerous individual factual truths—effective and conflicting, uncertain and ungraspable . . . One thing seems sure to me: the more one goes beyond factual truth, the more evident the difficulties of communication and understanding become. (Bez., p. 48)

Siggi experiences this same doubt as to any certainty that transcends the purely factual, and this is the essence of his own past experience, which has taught him that such fixed views and final judgements create only a seeming permanence in a world of changing reality, and are often the basis of

59

blind prejudice and closed minds. It is from this that guilt stems, the failure to realise the short-comings of one's rationally imposed view of the world, and failure to reassess constantly what appear to be truths. Such problems of reality are not ontological but moral, since it is in the moral sphere where opinions diverge on the same factual truths.

Siggi's past is fraught with such problems, which he must come to terms with as a representative of a generation. His past life, which begins at the age of nine in the narrative, is set in the North German coastal region, the fictional Rugbüll. His father is the local village policeman, a stubborn defender of middle-class virtues, and the agent of law and order in this microcosm of Nazi Germany. Set against him is the artist Max Ludwig Nansen (based partly upon the figure of the German Expressionist painter, Emil Nolde, whose real name was Hansen). A conflict arises when the work of the artist Nansen is proscribed by the Nazi authorities and he is forbidden to continue painting. Siggi's father, Ole Jepsen, has to issue and enforce the interdict and is later ordered to confiscate paintings. Through the figure of the policeman, Jepsen, Lenz demonstrates a perverted sense of duty, and points to this as the single most important feature of a social ethos which can allow and perpetuate the political iniquities of a dictatorial régime such as that of the Nazi state. The violence, atrocities and intimidation of Nazi Germany do not enter this remote region, but in their place there is the mentality of a German generation who forfeited a sense of *personal* responsibility and subordinated themselves to a state authority whose validity they never questioned. The notion of duty, central to the ethics of Kant and the German Idealist tradition, is here seen in a perversion of the original concept, and it points to the political immaturity of a nation that could suspend all rational moral judgement and embrace a belief in absolute authority as the basis of social organisation.

Only with mild reluctance does Jepsen perform his duty when first ordered to deliver the proscriptive letter, a reluctance that stems from a lifelong friendship with the artist and a feeling of indebtedness, since the latter had, at some time in the past, saved his life. But Siggi's father's reluctance and any sense of personal inclination is suppressed beneath his impersonal function:

> He kept finding things that would postpone his duty until, with annoyed amazement, he realised that he had turned into something new, that he had become a regulation policeman who needed nothing more to complete his orders than his bicycle, which was leaning against a sawing-trestle, in the shed. (D., p. 19)

In his uniform he extinguishes personal feelings and becomes an embodiment of the authority he represents; he is an agent of repression and a complete automaton. So predictable and absolute is his subordination to this authority that he even involuntarily buttons his uniform before answering the telephone. Unlike some of Lenz's work, where the individual succumbs to a superior force, in the face of a threat or out of moral weakness, Jepsen is seen as incapable of personal moral decisions. Berlin, where the orders originate, or Husum, where his immediate superiors are situated, appear remote, and their authority is communicated mainly by telephone or letter. Only occasionally do sinister figures, referred to simply as 'Ledermäntel' (leather trench-coats), intrude and remind one of a more brutal reality beyond the bounds of this circumscribed region. Jepsen is not intimidated, but neither does he have any ideological belief in the rightness of the course he is ordered to take; he is simply sure of the one fact, that authority must be obeyed.

Siggi's father does not understand why Nansen's work is banned, and excuses his own involvement in the business:

> My father realised that he owed Nansen something, so he said, 'I didn't think this up Max, you can believe me. I haven't anything to do with this professional ban, I only have to deliver it.' (D., p. 31)

But this, initially apologetic, attitude hardens into personal enmity as Nansen resists Jepsen's attempt to enforce the ban and later to confiscate pictures. Nansen represents the opposite pole. Jepsen is the embodiment of externally imposed duty, to the complete negation of the self and personal inclination, until the very purpose of his life becomes the pursuit of his duty: 'Without orders he was only half a man.' (D., p. 53). The artist, by contrast, becomes the embodiment of artistic freedom, of an inner duty, the expression of individual conviction and inclination which will bear no restraint from any outside authority. This is symbolically summed up at the moment of final confrontation between the two: the artist gestures with a defiant fist, while the policeman retains a posture of military obedience.

From this point the father becomes unshakeable in the stubborn defence of his duty. Warned that times might change, he simply dismisses the implications: 'When one does one's duty one need have no worries—even if times should change.' (D., p. 95). He has a similarly limited view of his responsibility with regard to the present. What happens in Berlin does not concern him, since he is 'only responsible for Rugbüll'. (D., p. 95). Nor does he question the reason for the ban imposed on Nansen, though he repeats the explanation given by his superiors:

> In the orders it says that he is alienated from the *Volk* . . . therefore he's a danger to the state and undesirable, just degenerate—if you know what I mean. (D., p. 95)

Jepsen's wife, in contrast, recognises and supports the ideological objections to Nansen's art:

> When you see the sort of people he paints, these green faces with Mongol eyes, deformed bodies, all this foreignness. He must be sick to paint like that. You don't see any German faces in his paintings . . . Just look at the faces of these people, twisted and black, they're either screaming or singing, not a single sensible word comes out of these mouths, at least not a German word. (D., p. 162)

Jepsen does not reflect on such matters, but is simply adamant that one must act in accordance with state author-

ity, even though this authority may be on the point of collapse:

> I don't ask what one has to gain by doing one's duty, whether it
> can benefit one, or anything like that. Where would we be if we
> asked ourselves at every turn: what happens after this? One can't
> do one's duty according to one's mood, or when caution pre-
> scribes it, if you understand me. (D., p. 260)

Even when it is obvious that the German capitulation is
imminent and the first allied troops have entered the region,
Jepsen calls out the home guard, consisting of the three other
adult males of the district, and forces them to set up a last line
of defence:

> He announced that there were orders, that these orders weren't
> there for nothing but had to be carried out, and to the letter,
> which meant in this case defending the road. (D., pp. 271–2)

Nansen, who initially complies with this, gradually tires of
this useless exercise and wishes to retire for the night, which
leads to a war of nerves as Jepsen threatens to shoot him for
deserting his post. The latter has to concede, however, and is
abandoned by the others to his night's vigil. Nansen already
sees the permanence of Jepsen's attitude and his inability to
change or to recognise the changes that are imminent:

> Nothing, not even the end, will change you. We'll have to wait
> until you are all dead. (D., p. 281)

The truth of this becomes evident after the end of the war.
After three months' internment for 'denazification', Jepsen
returns to his post, puts the new police regulations, unread,
in a drawer, and carries on unchanged and unrepentant. The
removal of the issuing authority does not cancel out the duty
previously prescribed, a duty that has become a personal
mission because of Nansen's stubborn resistance. Thus he
continues to confiscate and burn the artist's paintings. The
previous conflict of duty and reason becomes apparent in this
pathological state and against the changing historical background. The irrationality of his previous action is confirmed

when what had been a politically sanctioned activity becomes an absurd aberration, which he pursues with apparent immunity, though the father's future fate is left open in the novel.

Siggi's relationship with his father, who demands similar unquestioning obedience from him, is brought into conflict with a second father figure, Nansen, for whom the young Siggi feels a personal affection.

Jepsen attempts to inculcate in Siggi the same sense of duty, which he enforces through punishment. The father represents, within the family, the same dictatorial power as that of the state. He tries to use Siggi in his personal campaign against Nansen, using him as a spy:

> You don't need to understand any more than you are told, that's enough, do you understand me? . . . useful people have to submit . . . we'll make something useful of you, you'll see . . . We'll work together Siggi. I need you. You'll help me. No one can be a match for the two of us—not even him. You'll work for me and I'll make something proper out of you. (D., pp. 53–4)

But Siggi does not obey his father, and is drawn instead to Nansen, who enlists his help in hiding some paintings from his father's persecution.

Siggi respects and admires the artist Nansen, who exerts a formative influence upon him. It is through Nansen that Siggi learns to question reality, to see life as a dynamic process and not as a static, finalised state of being. Siggi attempts to protect Nansen's work from his father. However, just as his father's duty persists after the war, to the point that he burns down an old mill (which had been Siggi's secret hiding place, his retreat from the world) because some of Nansen's work had been hidden there, so too now a pathological trait emerges in Siggi. He has hallucinations in which he sees a flame threatening the paintings and feels an irrational compulsion to save them. He begins to steal and hide Nansen's paintings and later to steal paintings from public places, and this continues until his arrest and confinement in the corrective institution. Siggi is a parallel to his father: having assumed a stand against him, he continues this despite the changed circumstances, develops a fixed view and fails to see the reality that deviates from it. He too has developed a false sense of (self-imposed) duty. At this point he becomes like his father of whom he had said earlier:

> I began to fear him, not because of his strength or his cunning or his stubbornness, but fear of the infallibility that dwelt in him . . . This fixed-gazed contentment. This terrible calm in him. (D., p. 325)

It is the experience of one's own rightness, the abandoning of questioning that Lenz equates with moral guilt, it is complacency and a forfeiting of one's freedom, a form of self-abuse.

The father's stubbornness destroys the whole family. The elder son, Klaas, who has committed an act of self-mutilation, is handed over to the authorities by his father, who justifies his action:

> He knew what I have to do, my duty, he knew it. We can't turn things back. We've put all the questions, all the necessary questions, and we've answered them, as best we could. (D., p. 192)

The theme of questioning is central to the work. It is from Nansen that Siggi first learned to question the nature of reality. The lesson is communicated through Nansen's artistic theory, which is a typically Expressionist one, demanding creative vision rather than neutral observation:

> I'll tell you: one begins to see when one stops playing the observer and invents that which one needs: this tree, this wave, this beach. (D., p. 298)

His art is absolute freedom, even from the physical laws of reality. This artistic view stands in contrast to the complacency of other characters in the novel. Nansen advises Siggi to see life in this dynamic, changing way:

> One must not stop at that which one has. One has to make new starts, again and again. As long as we do that we can expect

SIEGFRIED LENZ

something of ourselves. I was never satisfied, Siggi, and I would
advise you: be dissatisfied whenever possible. (D., p. 352)

Thus Nansen conceives of duty in a different manner to
Siggi's father:

If we have any moral commitment then it is to look
ahead . . . Who forces us to make final judgements? (D., p. 156)

Nansen resists Jepsen and the ban imposed upon him:

Good . . . if you believe that one has to do his duty, then I'll say
the opposite: one has to do something that offends against duty.
For me duty is blind arrogance. It is unavoidable that one does
something that is not required by it. (D., p. 154)

Nansen is thus compared to Siggi's father, and also to the
remainder of the community, who have limited horizons,
and are rooted in the reality of their local region. Although
Nansen feels a strong attachment to this, his home area, and
attempts to capture its moods in his paintings, his philosophy is visionary rather than parochial or communal.

After an illustrated talk given by a 'Heimatdichter' (a
regional poet), in which an idealised view of local life and the
war is presented, Siggi and his father stop at a local inn. Siggi
reflects on the arrogance of the people, their smugness, complacency and their blind belief in the superiority of their local
region and sense of permanence and belonging:

So we sat in the 'Wattblick', while in Külkenwarf, I'm sure, they
were proving that their home by the sea was able to provide
answers to all the questions. All the questions. Why are our
people afraid to admit their ignorance now and again? The
greatest limitation that a sense of regional belonging leads to is
that one feels competent to answer all the questions: the arrogance of limited horizons. (D., p. 121)

This blind superiority is visible in their attitudes. They
dismiss the Americans as a rootless people, a wandering tribe
who live 'without lasting commitments, in a temporary
manner'. (D., p. 118) This belief in permanence and the
Germanic people, fixed in a timeless natural home, the

'healthy' ideal of the local idyll, is also implicit in Siggi's mother's attitude, who often seems to be the instigator of her husband's actions. She rejects her daughter Hilke's fiancé because he is a musician, calling him a gypsy. She also feels no compassion for his illness, epilepsy, and turns him out of the house because such weak blood is undesirable in a healthy German family. Similarly, in the post-war years, she warns Siggi against going near a home for mentally defective children:

> These worthless creatures . . . Now if they were ill, but no, they're worthless, they're a burden to us all . . . Just looking at them is enough to do you damage, Siggi, you don't notice it and suddenly there it is. Impressions, you know, they can stay in your mind and cloud your view. (D., pp. 341–2)

The themes of sight and blindness, health and illness run throughout the work. Those who claim unproblematic, healthy understanding are invariably those whose minds are closed to wider realities.

The unregenerate attitude which the mother demonstrates, voicing views entirely consistent with those of Nazi ideology, continues in other figures, though less is seen of them in the post-war years. They remove the lapel badges and the trappings of the previous ideology, but they remain essentially the same.

Siggi's parents continue to spurn his brother Klaas because of his previous misdemeanours and because he has not apologised for the shame he brought on the family, even though now his act need no longer be viewed as illegal. The father holds a trial, finds him guilty *in absentia*, bans him from the house and forbids his name ever to be mentioned again. A similar attitude is shown towards the daughter Hilke when it is discovered that she has posed, semi-nude, for Nansen. Their prudish moral indignation at this is heightened by the fact that it was Nansen, the family enemy, who painted her:

> Him, with his own laws, with his arrogance and his scorn for people who just do their duty. (D., p. 357)

67

Pernicious prejudice, coupled with a blind certainty that fails to take account of changing circumstances, or to take a wider view of the world—such are the experiences of Siggi's youth. In comparison to these figures he, at the end of his account, has not found an easy answer, has avoided final judgements and would like to rewrite his account, because of the danger that he might have 'seen' it wrongly here. Where others have certainty and all the answers, he is left with only questions:

> I ask why they look down so much on the sick . . . And I ask why they leave the stranger outside and scorn his help. And why they find it impossible to abandon some course and think of a better one . . . why they are so obsessed with the pursuit of a self-imposed task, this I ask. The silent voracity, the self-righteousness, the studied parochialism, this I question. And I question the way they walk, and stand, and look, and talk, and I cannot be satisfied with what I discover. (D., pp. 412–3)

Siggi is left without a mentor in his questioning; he concludes his account:

> I have nothing more to say, I have only questions left, which no one can answer, not even the painter, not even him. (D., p. 414)

Siggi distances himself from the figure who had previously appeared to be exemplary. This alienation is not simply attributable to the fact that Nansen showed no understanding when Siggi developed abnormally in the post-war years. Clearly during the period of suppression Nansen retained his personal integrity despite intimidation. But from this time he has not developed. What had previously been an admirable quality, the resistance to external pressure and the self-imposed inner duty of an ethical imperative, turns later into complacency. He has betrayed that commitment to 'dissatisfaction' that he had previously recommended to Siggi. He becomes a celebrated personality in art circles and allows this international recognition to distort his own philosophy of discontent. At an exhibition of his work he reacts to an art critic's eulogy with approval. Siggi 'saw that what amazed him most was his agreement with the critic's speech.' (D., p. 378) Yet to others present Nansen appears absurd: 'He's not true, he's invented himself.' (D., p. 379) He is, it is suggested, a living anachronism, better suited to a folklore museum than post-war Hamburg.

Siggi recognises this fault in one of Nansen's paintings displayed in the exhibition. Three masks hang suspended over a garden which they appear to threaten. Siggi is horrified by the impression that 'a terrible certainty radiated from them, an enigmatic certitude'. (D., p. 380) The masks, and the certainty, may be said to represent Siggi, Jepsen and Nansen. Each develops a sure conviction of what is demanded of them and refuses to revise this view of themselves.

It is shortly after this realisation of the artist's failure to adhere to his own ideals that Siggi, in a dream sequence, sees himself with a herd of seals being pursued by his father and Nansen. When they catch him they force him through a hoop, like animal trainers. The image reflects Siggi's (and Lenz's) view of the world as one of powerful determining forces, where people are forced into moulds of others' making. In the play *Das Gesicht* a reference is made to all educational processes, forms of instruction, and leadership as tyranny:

> It begins with the professions: fathers, teachers, experts: tyrannical professions. And he who is against me— (Ges., p. 64)

The certainty with which views are imposed on others is regarded as the starting point for intolerance and prejudice.

Siggi also experiences such attitudes among the younger generation. Whilst visiting his brother Klaas in Hamburg he comes into contact with a group of Bohemian pseudo-artists. A discussion of and fundamental disagreement on Nansen's work lead Siggi to criticise his older contemporaries: 'You condemn, and don't even take the trouble to understand.' (D., p. 389) Siggi's criticism is not valued, and he is knocked senseless by one of the group. Despite the most striking differences between this group and the older generation, differences that are stressed in the chaotic state of the flat they live in, as compared to the domestic order of life among the previous generation, similar mentalities are evident. Youth flaunts the conventions of its elders, but beneath this apparent call for tolerance from others lies a crude egoism. Arrogant self-assertion, certainty of one's own case, and the refusal to accept the validity of others' views are common features among the characters in the novel.

This same certainty is found in the figures who are in charge of the reformatory. This is demonstrated not only by the title of the essay that is the subject of Siggi's account of his own childhood, but in other essay themes such as 'Only he who can obey can give orders' (D., p. 405) which is only a slight variation on the opening lines of the Nazi poet Josef Weinheber's poem 'Gehorsam' (Obedience), part of a cycle entitled *Die deutschen Tugenden im Kriege* (German Virtues in the War).[25]

The traditional German virtues of duty, obedience and the value of hard work are the main points of this process of re-education. Meanwhile the head of the institution installs a piano in his office and composes *Lieder* to the Elbe, in the German Romantic tradition. For Siggi the Elbe has no such idealised associations, its passage symbolises to him the historical continuity of life which, 'even if he closes his eyes, still flows' (D., p. 7), and the amoral forces of life which devours its victims with innocent indifference. (D., p. 137) The conservatism of the reformatory is moderated with slight concessions to a more modern approach by the intro-duction of psychologists to give some scientific insight to the abnormalities of the inmates.

Siggi believes that the correction is being applied to the wrong generation, and that he like the others is being punished for the moral disorientation caused by a previous generation. The psychologists invent jargon to offer rational explanations for life's casualties, but these are dismissed as the excuse of a society that cannot see its own faults.

The description of Siggi's life can be seen as an inverted form of the *Bildungsroman*. Traditionally such novels end with the integration of the hero into society when he reaches a mature view of the world. But such naive optimism is absent from this novel. Siggi, who reaches the age of majority whilst in the reformatory, attains greater maturity than the society he lives in, and realises that his past experience has not educated him towards life, but away from it; he emerges as the outsider, not as the integrated member of society.

This use of the outsider as offering a novel perspective on life, and the relationship of German past and present, can also be found in other modern novels such as Grass's *Die Blechtrommel* (The Tin Drum), with which Lenz's work has many other parallels, and Böll's *Ansichten eines Clowns* (The Clown). Lenz, however, reinforces the central character's account of his past life by the introduction of other perspectives. Siggi abandons himself totally to his own past, and allows his former self to tell the story. He views his own past almost in the form of a film, eager to allow his characters to justify their actions, rather than impose a judgement on them. This technique of neutral observer and first-person narrator presents technical problems that Lenz encounters in earlier novels, particularly when he has his narrator report incidents which he did not witness, as well as his indispensable, but improbable presence on many other occasions.

In this novel Lenz introduces a second perspective through the figure of the psychologist Mackenroth, who wishes to investigate Siggi's case as the subject of an academic thesis. Mackenroth, unlike the other psychologists, places the burden of guilt on society and researches Siggi's past life to prove this. But Mackenroth's 'scientific' investigation proves more biased than Siggi's objective report, and interprets facts to support a preconceived idea, that of a deprived child, starved of affection, in a world of shifting values.

Siggi rejects Mackenroth's findings because they are simply an attempt to provide extentuating circumstances that would excuse his action. He does not want to be seen simply as the abnormal psychological product of an environment in which he was starved of parental love, torn between two father figures, alienated from his school friends, confused as to right and wrong by the conflict he became involved in, and from which he emerged with an obsession prompted by hallucinations. Whilst he accepts that his development was socially qualified, he considers the pathological aspect of his later self not an individual psychological manifestation but a characteristic feature of those people he was brought up with. He believes that Mackenroth has reduced the problem 'to a too convenient opposition' (D., p. 371) and attempts to explain his problem more fully by referring to his visit to the Hamburg gallery, where he first recognised Nansen in a changed light, and his confrontation with the pseudo-artist Hansi. His own development into an art thief he considers as a parallel to such attitudes.

A third perspective is also introduced by the figure of a warder in the reformatory, Joswig. He attempts to clarify Siggi's difficulties in discussing the pleasures of duty with a parable in which he shows how genuine duty is victorious over baser instinct. Though Siggi accepts that there may be times when a clear sense of right and wrong exists, and personal inclination must be subordinated to a higher moral imperative, such a naive view of life ignores the past abuses of such concepts:

> Those are the pleasures of duty as Korbjuhn [the German master] would like them, but the victims of duty are something else, we don't talk about them. (D., p. 316)

Yet Joswig is possibly the most positive character in the novel. He appears to be able to strike a balance between the duty imposed on him by authority and his ability to interpret this in his own way, occasionally disregarding regulations. But this relatively minor character is the only positive figure in an otherwise bleak and pessimistic world.

However, it would be wrong to see the strengths and the

success of the novel simply in its theme. The central action of the novel, pared of the detail that accompanies it, is only a small part of the overall work. The narrative tone and the quality of the many descriptive passages are important features that explain the work's appeal. The use of a child narrator allows Lenz the freedom to combine imagination and irony with descriptive realism. The amount of detail occasionally detracts from the main narrative, and many episodes make little contribution to the development of the theme. Yet such detail serves the function of creating a mood of objective authenticity in the mature Siggi's report of his earlier life. The natural descriptions which evoke the harsh, severe landscape of the North German coastal region serve more than a decorative function. The very mood of the region is brought to life, and is an atmosphere that seems to contribute to the regional mentality.

The war-time background seems almost incidental to the novel. It emerges in some of Siggi's games, but here reduced to the level of attacks on sea-gulls and ducks, and in the occasional radio broadcast or newspaper headline, but the suffering of the war never enters the scope of the novel. Klaas is a victim, but only one other physical casualty is mentioned, whilst the only fatality is a cow that has to be slaughtered when hit by shrapnel.

But if physical victims are lacking, mental ones are not, and this applies to most of the central characters. Siggi fails to adapt to the changed circumstances after the war. This required change is not some kind of opportunism, such as that of the former Nazi art critic Maltzahn, who tries to curry favour with Nansen, excusing his past assessment of the artist's work and his 'temporary misunderstanding', but a return to a state of questioning.

Lenz communicates his theme almost incidentally amidst the profusion of detail and through the perspective of the child. Chapter 4, 'The Birthday', seems in part simply childish fantasy, as Siggi, present but hardly partaking in the festivities, turns the assembled company into species of marine creatures, with protruding eyes, voracious appetites and a seeming detachment from the world about them. It is not until much later that the 'silent voracity' (D., p. 412) of this and other domestic scenes emerges not as a childish impression prompted by exclusion from the adult circle, but as an indication of the mentality of the local people. Their physical appetite is seen as typical of their unproblematic certainty, and their unreflective capacity to consume life. It is in such features, as well as the ideological certainty of a historical period, as propounded by Siggi's biology teacher in the form of social Darwinism, that Siggi sees the faults of his people.

Faced with this past experience of others' certainty and his fear of any form of positive conviction or unquestioning acceptance, Siggi can only consider a withdrawal from the world as the adequate response to its challenge which forces one towards commitment.

Lenz has created in this work a strong reminder of the German past and the faults of a society that he regards as having failed to grasp the lessons of that past. Yet the moral of the story may apply equally well to any society and to regard it, and the problem of duty, simply as the German virtue that became the German vice, is to assume a moral certainty about ourselves that Lenz warns against. Lenz presents man as seeking after certainty, which he may find, but only at the risk of losing the highest freedom, the freedom to doubt.

5

DAS VORBILD

That Lenz's most recent novel should bear the title *Das Vorbild* (An Exemplary Life, 1973) might lead one to expect a new departure in his work: the title would seem to indicate the commitment to some positive hero, and an escape from the moral disorientation and failure of the central character in so many of his others works. But this is not the case. Like *Deutschstunde*, it centres on the problem of the certainty of moral attitudes, and the way in which they can constitute a form of tyranny over those exposed to them. Lenz sets out, not to portray an exemplary figure, but to reiterate his conviction that there is no patent prescription for the individual's rôle in society. Where anything of the kind is found, it is shown to be the defective, or at best myopic vision of the prejudiced mind. The exemplary in life is not that which offers a solution, but rather that which prompts questioning: 'An exemplary character should not anaesthetise but stimulate doubt.' (Vor., p. 487)

Formally, this novel demonstrates a tendency that is present in all Lenz's work, the use of moral debate as the structuring element. This is seen most clearly in the setting of a committee-meeting as the fictional background. The three central characters meet to discuss material for inclusion in a school reader. Having completed such apparently uncontroversial topics as 'Work and Holidays' and 'Other Lands and Ours' (here Lenz's irony is apparent), they are struggling with the theme 'Biography and Exemplary Lives'.

The three (most unlikely) educationalists are set the task of choosing a passage or story that would present a figure worthy of emulation by the younger generation. But, within the course of this discussion, these fictional characters are subjected to the author's scrutiny and their competence and suitability as moral arbiters, as well as the validity of their undertaking are brought into question.

The biographical background of the three figures is developed to reveal them as in need of greater moral guidance than the children they are potentially advising. The inability of the group to agree on some model figure is anticipated from the outset; each has a differing political attitude and they have fundamentally divergent views on the educational process in which they are involved. Further, each is as intransigent in defence of his own conviction as the others, an attitude reflected in the observation:

> 'How difficult it is to convince others, and how cheerless to be convinced by others oneself.' (Vor., p. 13)

By means of three sub-plots, a number of minor characters and various interpolated stories (these being the excerpts that are under discussion), Lenz employs his technique of using different perspectives to present variations on the same theme. The method is not so successful as in *Deutschstunde*, and the reader is constantly aware of its artificiality, despite the author's attempt to introduce a tone of irony into the manipulation of his fictional characters through the third person narrative.

Lenz has been criticised for the level of discussion in the novel which, it is maintained, does not reflect that of educational debate in modern Germany. Such criticism fails to recognise the point that he simply employs the debate as a fictional means of considering not institutionalised educational methods, but rather the general transmission of social attitudes. That Lenz's concern is the general restructuring of society is evident in his use here of a recurrent symbolism of houses under reconstruction or renovation, requiring the support of scaffolding—the ideological equivalent of which these three compilers are to supply with their new reader.

The stultifying effect of the educational process is suggested first by the conference-room setting. The building was constructed before the First World War, and the room itself is oppressive, dark and gloomy, and decorated with African weapons from a colonial past. The building might be said to represent a 'Victorian' belief in human progress and perfectibility and the optimism stemming from the years of the foundation of Bismarck's Reich. The experience of two world wars and the collapse of German society have not, Lenz suggests, brought about a fundamental shift in attitudes. As in *Deutschstunde*, he shows us the process of reconstruction on the foundations of the German past, with all its inherent structural weaknesses.

But the three committee members are not themselves illustrations of traditionalist complacency. They represent three distinct social attitudes. Valentin Pundt is the conservative voice of authoritarianism, the traditionalist. A retired headmaster from the remote region of the Lüneburg Heath, his world is circumscribed and hermetic, and this is symbolised in his objection to the draughts in the conference-room, which he hunts out and stops up. Janpeter Heller is the revolutionary, progressive teacher, who despises all forms of authority, other than his own; his militancy is symbolised by his fascination with the African weapons, by the faded red jumper he wears and by his 'provocative' beard which, because of a receding chin, refuses to make him look as revolutionary as he would like to be. Rita Süssfeldt represents the liberal voice. She acts as a conciliatory figure between the two extremes, but is herself ineffectual. She tends naturally to Pundt's opinions but is drawn back to the centre by Heller. *Distraite*, disorganised, and dishevelled, she is unable to cope with the most mundane aspects of her own life. Her attitude is symbolised in her complete disregard for traffic regulations in the centre of Hamburg, through which she drives with a careless disregard for the danger to which she exposes herself, her passengers and the public as well.

The incompatibility of the three characters is reflected in

the passages which they put forward and the interpretations they place upon them. Heller suggests the story of a son who rejects a lucrative, but dishonest, living offered him by his father. The father, a doctor employed by the Social Security Board to assess claimants' entitlement to a disability pension, is open to bribery. The son rejects the father's offer and becomes a ship's doctor. Heller's story is turned down because it is too negative and suggests a false sense of responsibility, the wish 'to retain the luxury of a good conscience by simply not becoming involved'. (Vor., p. 43) There is an echo of Lenz's own views in the last remark, and it is there too in Heller's reply, which attacks the very concept of the traditional heroic, ideal figure:

> Ideal characters are a sort of pedagogic cod-liver oil, which everyone takes with a feeling of revulsion, or at least with their eyes closed. They repress the young, make them insecure and irritable . . . one should be dealing with the every-day, not the ideal. (Vor., p. 45)

Heller maintains that excellence is 'asocial', since 'no one can feel solidarity with someone who is excellent.' (Vor., p. 64) Such a view is ideologically qualified: traditional exemplary characters create the impression that man is by nature immoral and that only by overcoming his real nature can he attain any degree of social acceptability. This view is a distortion of the fact that environmental conditions can force man to become immoral. For Heller, their task ought to consist in illustrating that

> each can become his own ideal—if given the chance to realise his latent potential . . . and how this latent potential, or that hindered by circumstances, could be realised. (Vor., p. 107)

It emerges that the suggestions are, in fact, little more than an idealised projection of the committee members' own lives. Heller has rejected the 'suspect' security of marriage in order to dedicate himself to the ideological battle. Pundt, who offers the tale of a soldier who helps an escapee despite the latter's ingratitude, reflects his own life (as he sees it), as an educator of ungrateful pupils. Süssfeldt's example of a mother who pawns her engagement ring in order to provide money for her son (who has escaped from a reformatory) but who later informs the police, is a commentary on her own abivalent attitude towards her cousin Heino Merkel, an attitude that varies between self-sacrifice and rejection. Each is looking for confirmation of his or her own life through these examples—but the 'model life' that each puts forward is still flawed.

In the course of the novel, the faults of the three committee-members themselves are revealed, and they are, ironically, subjected to an educational process. Their project appears to be on the verge of failure when they discover the biography of Lucy Beerbaum, a scientist born in Greece, who had emigrated to Germany and become a Professor of Biology, researching into the DNA molecule, which controls heredity. Most memorable in her life is her action of solidarity and sympathy with Greek dissidents arrested by the military junta. She imposes upon herself a similar form of arrest, subjecting herself to the same privations, with severe restrictions on food and visits. As a result, her physical condition is weakened, she contracts pneumonia and dies.

The group investigates her life, and they reach a measure of agreement, though this is due not so much to what they have read as to the personal crises that they experience during the investigation. The personal problems, combined with the forced reassessment of the characters they had suggested as examples, serve to undermine the fixed views they had of themselves. Again, as in *Deutschstunde*, the inability to change one's views is seen as a form of complacency that can endanger the individual.

Pundt is in search of information about his son Harald, who commits suicide for no apparent reason after achieving a distinction in his university examinations. In investigating his son's past, Pundt discovers himself, and becomes aware of his own share of responsibility for his son's death. He

SIEGFRIED LENZ

begins to see himself through other people's eyes. He learns that his son, and other pupils, referred to him as 'the sign-post . . . which only pointed one way' (Vor., p. 58), and that his educational method consisted solely in 'breaking others' wills' (Vor., p. 215), forcing them to conform to his own. He had brought up his son in a tyrannical manner, requiring him to account for every moment of his time and justify every action. Pundt had tried to inculcate in his son and his pupils the certainty of his own views, refusing to admit even of doubt or compromise. He had referred to the 'dignity of persistence', explaining that 'we must see our plans through, not turn back, even at the risk of making mistakes.' (Vor., p. 147). Lenz returns here to the theme of *Deutschstunde*, and the son's suicide may be compared with Siggi's despair at the end of the novel. Pundt now realises that his concept of education was really nothing more than intimidation. As happened in *Deutschstunde*, the son develops aspects of the father's personality. Faced with the prospect of becoming a teacher himself, he realises the potential abuse inherent in the rôle. His fixation—inherited from his father—with rationalising everything imposes excessive demands on his rigorously logical mind, and he discovers that the questions simply cannot be answered. Harald emerges as a tragic example of modern life, although he is not exemplary in the positive sense but in the illustrative.

His suicide cannot be blamed solely upon his father; disillusionment with his contemporaries appears to be a contributory factor as well. Like Siggi Jepsen, Harald develops an obsession that is similar in intensity, if not in object, to that of his father. He turns into a figure of protest rather than one of persistent acceptance; a symbolic comparison with his father is made by a reference to the fact that Harald's favourite seat was always under the ventilator. It is suggested that his commitment to protest was so obsessive and so consistent, that no form of action could be ruled out—not even suicide.

A disillusionment with protest brings in yet another potentially exemplary figure, the pop-star Mike Mitchner, idol of the adolescents. Harald had been attached to Mitchner in his days as a protest singer, whom he admired as the most effective spokesman of their various causes:

> We were not prepared to see the world as a finalised fact, with these judges, these fathers, these consumers and these bosses—you gave voice to our revolt. (Vor., p. 312)

But Mitchner was seduced by success, became a pop-star and abandoned his protest, allowing himself to be exploited by commercial interests, and hailed by the press as the 'singer of a healthy world' (Vor., p. 313) where protest was not needed. Significantly, the frame in which Harald had kept Mitchner's photograph is found empty in his room.

Mitchner *is* an exemplary figure, one who can be accepted as such by a section of modern youth, but his value is questionable. He is an opiate to his fans, 'the priest of the guitar, who proselytises for the religion of self-oblivion'. (Vor., p. 274) Through Pundt, Lenz describes the mass hysteria of a pop-concert, and the fans attempt to experience a kind of *unio mystica* with this messianic figure. (Vor., p. 67) Their reaction is a parallel to Harald's suicide, in that they too are striving for some form of negation of the self. Lenz's presentation of modern youth is not particularly favourable. They are either pop-fans looking for a new religion, or asocial thugs, or recalcitrant protesters. The historical reasons which underly the emergence of such a generation are never clearly defined, though the general theme of the novel suggests reaction against the previous generation as the answer.

Pundt withdraws from the committee, realising that he is not a fit person to recommend ideals to others. Though he never refers to it as a reason, it seems obvious that the fact that he was beaten up by a group of muggers whilst trying to help another couple who were being attacked, contributes to his decision. The experience makes clear the immense gap between the young people in the real world, and the objects of the abstract debate upon which the committee is engaged.

81

Heller undergoes a similar process of self-realisation in the course of the novel. When it opens, his marriage is in ruins, and he has become estranged from his wife because of his political views and his selfishness. All attempts at reconciliation founder on his inability to communicate with her. Eager for recognition and for the approval of others, he ingratiates himself with his own pupils by embracing their causes as his own. His speech and manners are characterised by the clichés and the jargon of the far left. His political posturings are reflected in his refusal to take flowers when visiting Süssfeldt, a convention he castigates as 'an inherited German bad habit' (Vor., p. 195), and he criticises his wife for buying him a desk—he regards this as the first sign of the bourgeois obsession with property. His greatest fault is his immaturity. Yet in spite of all the implicit criticism, there is a certain similarity between some of his attitudes and views voiced by Lenz in some of the early works:

> In the name of the unsuspecting pupils I must protest against the way in which in an attitude of typical conformity to the system, you try to give our pupils an inferiority complex by making them live in front of stifling monuments. (Vor., p. 103)

The inferiority seems to be felt primarily by Heller. To the detriment of his home-life, he dedicates his whole time to the ideological enlightenment of his pupils. He seeks the outside approval that he wants so much in the quarter in which he can most easily make an impression—the half-formed minds of the young. His wife points this out to him:

> Oh Jan, you act as if you were one of them. You talk like them, you dress like them, you play up to them as if their approval were the only thing that mattered. They admire you and you repay them by forgetting what distinguishes you from them. It's pathetic, Jan, it really is. (Vor., p. 189).

That his actions are also to some extent a compensation for his feelings of sexual inadequacy is suggested too, in the many attempts to assert himself sexually with Magda, the

82

exotic maid, and in his generally erotic imagination (Vor., p. 193).

Heller provides another example of extreme intransigence, not realising that his own attitude is as intolerant as that of the people he opposes. Lenz points out the similarity neatly, although it goes unnoticed by Heller himself. Driving along with Süssfeldt, he comments on the use of advertising catch-phrases and the pervasive, manipulative effect of the language they use. Yet a moment later he becomes involved in a pupils' demonstration against fare increases on public transport, the chanted rallying-cry of which has precisely the same features as the advertising catch-phrase. Heller not only joins the demonstration, but is soon heading it, and is happy to be arrested. He is unmoved by the policeman's reference to him:

> Mr Heller, in case no one has pointed it out before, I'd like to tell you something. As long as I've been on this job, I've never come across anything so pathetic as an ageing revolutionary. (Vor., p. 122)

Only gradually does Heller's attitude change, as he becomes aware of its psychological foundation, and of his own intolerance. No clear indication of the watershed is given, but the turning-point seems to come when he attempts a confrontation with his wife's lover, a doctor. As he examines Heller—and at the same time resists attempts by the latter to provoke him into a showdown—the doctor receives a telephone call to tell him that one of his patients has died, partly because of a wrong diagnosis on his part. The significance of the incident is suggested later by Pundt, who unwittingly points to the similarities between the doctor and the three members of the committee: 'Doctors and pedagogues should make at least one mistake, but even that can be one too many.' (Vor., p. 459). The experience of fallibility is what had been lacking in them all.

Süssfeldt has erred in her attitude towards her cousin, Heino Merkel. This character places the concept of the exemplary figure into yet another perspective, this time a grotesque one. Merkel is obsessed with a feeling of guilt. A number of wild animals have been killed in a fire for which he feels responsibility; he was himself injured in the fire, and his brain has been damaged. When attacked by fits of madness, which are brought on by reading about animals, he feels compelled to release all the animals from the local zoo, and has, indeed, already done so on a number of occasions. Süssfeldt and her sister have installed a special chair in his room in which he can be confined when such attacks occur. The use of figures like Merkel to represent certain mental attitudes is not uncommon in Lenz's work, most notably in *Deutschstunde*. Past guilt or assumed guilt lead to a gesture of over-compensation: Merkel removes all restrictions and barriers and allows a natural anarchy to prevail—to the jeopardy of others. For all that, he still wishes to be able to restrain himself, to conquer his *idée fixe* and maintain a state of balance.

Süssfeldt incurs guilt through her treatment of her cousin. He feels under an obligation to her and to her sister, forced to submit to their pity in 'a life-long trap of gratitude'. (Vor., p. 220) The sisters derive satisfaction from the knowledge that their sacrifices are saving Merkel from a mental institution. Eager to give her cousin a feeling of self-respect, Süssfeldt also arranges that a literary prize committee, of which she is a member, should accept his nomination. When he discovers this ploy, he abandons his cousins, however, and attains the independence that he has been seeking. Süssfeldt's fault is that she sees everything in emotional terms, and that she wants the ability to perceive logical consequences for her actions. This is reflected in her remark that rational enquiry removes the mystery of life; she warns, in fact, against interpreting things too closely, lest 'we interpret our lives into enlightened boredom.' (Vor., p. 363) she recognises her fault when Merkel leaves, but this effectively removes, at the same time, the focus of her very existence.

The progress of the novel erodes any feelings on the part of

84

the central figures that their lives are somehow exemplary, but it does not explore the changes they undergo; we see only the rejection of some views held previously. No genuine examples emerge, then, from the trio or from the characters associated with them.

Some other, more incidental, characters in the novel underline the human need for examples that can be followed. There is the footballer, Charly Gurk, the idol of millions; there is Mr Meister, whose perfect smile is used in advertisements to illustrate the satisfaction that can be derived from the products advertised—a motif which echoes, in fact, one of Lenz's earliest short stories; there is, finally, a brief scene, watched through a window, of an apprentice working with a craftsman. Here the 'example' is being passed from one generation to the next. None of these, however, provided an adequate answer to the problem of finding an exemplary life for the school reader.

Ponderous conservatism, visionary ideology, sweet sympathy—the qualities are all suggested in part by the names of the central figures—prove in turn to be oppressive and potentially tyrannical. But the example finally chosen, Lucy Beerbaum, does not seem free of fault herself. The various excerpts presented from her life raise questions, and provoke the critical detachment that the selection committee come to see as essential in the evaluation of any 'exemplary' character. The episodes concerned all hinge upon acts of the individual conscience. Beerbaum accepts responsibility for tools and messages found in loaves of bread sent to a prison, in order to save the baker; she condones a rigged election by which she becomes student political representative, because she feels that she will be more effective than her moderate rival; she denies authorship of an article in a workers' newspaper, leaving others to face jail, because her continued contributions to the paper are more important that confessing the truth; and she abandons her commitment to scientific research in order to demonstrate her solidarity with the prisoners of the Junta.

The committee selects this last action, and in illustration of youth's reaction to her protest, they add the responses of her two nieces. One sees the act simply as futile. The other is inspired by it. Lucy Beerbaum's case exemplifies the conflict between inner and outer duty. Her scientific commitment, which Lenz is at pains to underline as being of vital importance, conflicts with her duty to bear witness to the abuse of political power. Unfortunately, though, Lenz blurs the issue. Lucy's rôle as a scientist implies a commitment to all of mankind (for all that, science, here seen on the verge of discovering the secret of human life, might also provide a basis for a new hubris on the part of man). Her solidarity with the Greek dissidents, moreover, might in fact arise from her sympathy for one single individual. Further, when her physical condition weakens, she breaks the self-imposed rules of her 'arrest', and permits herself medical attention.

How the reader is to interpret Lucy Beerbaum is unclear, and several questions remain unanswered: Is she exemplary through her very inconsistency? Does her protest have any value other than a personal or spiritual one? Is she not the embodiment of an obsessive and finally self-destructive duty? Lucy seems to exert an inspiring influence upon one of the nieces in a way that is not tyrannical; but the whole novel argues the point that any attempt to influence others—even through sympathy—is potentially intimidatory.

For the three selectors, the problem seems to be solved, however: they have found their 'shining example.' But when this chapter of the reader is submitted to the publisher, Lenz shows us another stubborn attitude. The publisher simply refuses to accept this life for his textbook. He proves to be more extreme than any of the other figures, and rejects Beerbaum as a misguided idealist:

> Protest against illegal violence, fine. But it's a private protest. Contemplative. Meditative. An elegaic 'no'. A protest in humility. An emancipatory education can't be satisfied with that—a protest without action and therefore without consequence. (Vor., p. 517)

He demands instead an active ideal, someone to 'stimulate the revolutionary potential in the schools'. (Vor., p. 518)

So the exercise is a failure. In a final ironic comment, Heller sends Pundt a picture-postcard of a windmill:

> Shortly before I left, we found the ideal for today's world. It's a windmill, completely intact, which, when there's enough wind, turns its sails for all to see. (Vor., p. 527)

Why a windmill? It has no intrinsic driving force, but it reacts to external stimuli in a predestined manner. But if the programmed movement of the windmill is the human conscience, when is it activated, and how does it react?

It was perhaps inevitable that criticism should be levelled at *Das Vorbild* after the great success of *Deutschstunde*. But the novel does have certain very clear flaws, not the least of which is the ambiguity of the final outcome. The central narrative is too fragmentary, and it does not arise, moreover, out of an inherent problem. Rather the reverse is true: the characters are constructed to suit the line of the debate. A strategy that can be employed successfully in the plays, say, tends to force this novel into an essayistic mould. Lenz has a good eye for comic detail and human eccentricity, but for all that, the didactic and somewhat heavy moralising of the debate dominates the work.

Unlike *Deutschstunde*, the novel is not set in the German past, nor, like others of his plays and novels, in some anonymous country. It is set in Germany in 1968. Although the central trio and the other characters do represent a number of modern attitudes, Beerbaum's life refers to problems in Greece, and to the 'extreme situation' imposed upon the individual by an authoritarian régime, motifs used by Lenz in many of his earlier works. Whilst many of the characters may be dismissed as examples in the illustrative sense, but not worthy of emulation, Beerbaum's case, intended to be provocative, does not in fact provoke questions that are of particular relevance to the society in which Lenz is writing. The problem, and the final ironic reference to the windmill,

87

hark back to *Stadtgespräch*, in which people react once again to the pressures of authoritarianism, but do so too late.

Lenz's iconoclasm leaves a vacuum. The abstract nature of the debate is in constant danger of losing sight of the object of the discussion. The development of the characters in the novel still leaves the reader with no indication of their future, but it is the future that is Lenz's main concern. We are left almost with the impression that the only truly exemplary life would be that of a recluse. But this is countered, too, by Lenz's view that to be uncontentious is not the same thing as to be innocent. The circular motion of the windmill seems to serve as symbol of Lenz's constant return to this single dilemma of human existence.

6

THE SHORT STORIES—I
FROM SULEYKEN TO BOLLERUP

In 1955 Lenz published his cycle of short stories *So zärtlich war Suleyken* (How Sweet was Suleyken), and the popularity of these twenty humorous tales is attested to by film versions, and by a profusion of gift editions, which include—significantly—both editions for children, and specially illustrated texts. Early criticism of Lenz tended to regard the stories as a unique phenomenon outside the mainstream of his work, but he has since published a parallel selection of North German village stories. Both deserve more critical attention than has been afforded to them.

Suleyken is a fictitious village in Masuria, that southern part of East Prussia where Lenz spent his childhood, and in an afterword to the collection Lenz speaks of the stories as a 'declaration of love for his country' (Sul., p. 149). Although the geographical features play some part, the character of the people of Suleyken is the centre of interest, and Lenz talks in the afterword of their 'basic intelligence', difficult for the outsider to grasp, but having in it elements of 'dazzling cunning, ponderous trickery, clumsy affection and an endearing patience' (Sul., p. 148). An essay published by Lenz some ten years after the stories, 'Lächeln und Geographie' (Smiles and Geography), expands the afterword, and speaks this time of the reluctance of the people of Masuria to make concessions to the world outside. Yet they are in themselves people of a 'lively simplicity' (Bez., p. 77).

In the tales themselves, the patience of the people of Suleyken, with most of whom the narrator claims to be related, plays a large part: indeed, whether the quality in

SIEGFRIED LENZ

question is patience, stoicism or stubbornness is debatable.
Hamilkar Schass, for example, having learned to read at the
age of seventy-one, refuses to be budged from his book by
enemy attack, and the intruder retires discomfited. The same
Hamilkar—and the names have a memorable outlandish-
ness about them—also acts for Suleyken in a dispute with
neighbouring Schissomir over the ownership of some
swamp-land claimed by both villages. This time Hamilkar
wins a conscious victory by making clear to the opponents
how long he is prepared to sit things out: he plants a supply of
onions and settles down. The second year is too much for
Schissomir.

A 'duel' between representatives of the same villages takes
place when two buggies are unable to pass each other on a
narrow road. Neither gives way, and the pair are eventually
removed with a crane. The same attitude to time recurs in
incidental motifs. Thus the commission sent to inoculate the
unwilling (and elusive) children of Jadwiga Plock settles
down for a long wait—one of their number even becomes
engaged during the stay. The fine line between patience and
stubbornness is demonstrated, too, in Hamilkar Schass's
conscription into the local fusiliers. Refusing to accept the
authority of the blustering commandant, he achieves the
aims (so far unfulfilled) of the fusiliers, namely the catching
of some smugglers, by his own means and in his own good
time, and, when he has had enough of the fusiliers, he leaves.

The world outside is avoided, and this normally includes
Schissomir and especially Striegeldorf, five stops away on the
local railway, an institution itself regarded with gravest sus-
picion. Thus when a smith needs a bag of nails the entire
population accompanies him in a procession, the end of
which is leaving Suleyken just as the vanguard arrives in
Oletzko. The *Fremde* (foreign parts) harbours threats, and it
is significant that the first and last of the tales deal with the
repulse of outside attackers. Other tales itemise the threats
involved. The inoculation and elementary hygiene forced
upon the numerous Plock children makes them ill, and only

when they revert to their former rather rustic eating habits do they recover, Adam Arbatzki dies when he is imprudent enough to take the medicine the doctor prescribed—an illustration, incidentally, of a type of joke that is familiar in a number of other contexts. But persons as diverse as the school inspector and a chicken thief are defeated because they cannot come to terms with Suleyken and its 'consistent illogicality'.[26] The local railway is a failure, and the brave talk of the promoter of the venture that 'America has become a step nearer' meets only the question: 'Why, dammit, do we all have to go to America? Isn't it all right here, too?' (Sul., p. 91).

The people of Suleyken are essentially unreflective, rarely thinking beyond the essentials of everyday living. In the school, digging a latrine takes precedence over mathematics. Some things are necessary, some are not. The railway promoter tries to draw from an onlooker the idea of christening the line:

> 'Adolf Abromeit, your wife, let's say, has a baby. A little fat fellow. Right. We've got that far. What, if you please, are you going to do with him?'
> 'Bath him,' shouted Adolf Abromeit.
> 'Right,' said the good gentleman. 'And then?'
> 'Feed him'.
> 'Right again. And what else?'
> 'Use a bit of powder..' (Sul., p. 89)

The promoter gives up and mentions the naming of the child himself. And the railway, in fact, receives the name Popp.

Neither characters nor authors are sentimental. Death is accepted entirely, and the funeral of Aunt Arafa, say, is in the tradition of the Irish wake, though fights are in fact avoided. Her demise (in a tale called 'A Lovely Funeral') provides a good example of local logic, the obvious humour which (coupled as it is with reader-superiority) makes for much of the entertainment. She dies *en route*, and must be brought across a border. Her two nephews are questioned:

'Why, dammit, is she so quiet?'

'She is, word of honour, asleep. And perhaps, Mr Captain Sir, we might request a little peace for a sleeping lady.'

'Of course,' said the officer, 'all well and good. But where is my guarantee that your dear blood-relation-aunt has not, as it might be, departed this life?'

'If she,' said the cousins, 'had departed this life, she would not be able to sleep; and our dear aunt is asleep.'

The officer pondered, and since the logic was acceptable, he let the coach through. (Sul., p. 47)

Nor is Adam Arbatzki—whose death has been noted already—mourned. 'Actually, he was about the right age for it.' (Sul., p. 115)

Equally, love is not a matter for sentimentality. Joseph Gritzan's courtship of Katherina is virtually wordless, but not in the tradition of the tongue-tied bumpkin. Joseph has put in a considerable amount of (literal) spadework at the house of the pastor to obtain a baptismal certificate. Armed with this and some liquorice he comes courting, and the social system of Suleyken accepts these as sufficient indication of an imminent wedding.

The response of the Suleyker to the supernatural is as practical as that to other emotional situations. Metaphysical phenomena are met with strictly earthly answers. When the late Adam Arbatzki haunts an apple tree (which refuses to be felled), to the discomfiture of his young widow, the answer is found of grafting on to the tree several other fruits, thus confusing the spirit out of existence. In the final tale, the hunter of a famous stag claimed by Suleyken is tricked by two villagers and an animal skin. When, after a long wait, the would-be hunter has the real beast pointed out to him, he will have nothing to do with it: 'You can't trust your own eyes here, Adam Przyball. Drive on . . .' (Sul., p. 147). These are the last words of the cycle, and they tie in with Lenz's serious considerations on the nature of observed truth in the novels. Here, though, the outsider simply cannot grasp the details of the world, and the child-analogy is quite appropriate.

Suleyken has a prophetess, however, for all that the magic brew in which she will see the future contains some unlikely ingredients (including a piece of sausage, later rescued, and a photograph). Her prognostications about the coming rifle-contest and fair are partly true, but the inquirer, Ludwig Karnickel, confesses afterwards to a certain amount of trouble making sure that all the prophecies take their proper course.

Two tales are central to the collection. The first shows Suleyken's reaction to a circus, and it is surely no accident that this was made the title-story to a selection for children, illustrated very well by Klaus Warwas. 'That's how it was with the Circus' demonstrates the naive–literal acceptance of illusion. A knifethrower is booed off, since that sort of thing isn't done in Suleyken. A magician who produces a rabbit ostensibly from the coat of Stanislaw Griegull loses this prop to Stanislaw. The strong man, finally, is outwitted by the local weakling.

The second tale concerns the argument between Zoppek, a fisherman and swimmer, and Kuckuck, a shoemaker. Arguments in Suleyken are taken seriously, but their matter is sometimes confusing—we hear, for example, of a debate (won by Griegull) on the Christian names of Napoleon. Zoppek has argued here that the Prussian knights would have made it beyond East Prussia into Russia had they only possessed bicycles. Humour lies in the unexpected response, and this is what we get from Kuckuck. 'How, if you please, can you possibly know whether the knights would have been able to mend punctures?' (Sul., p. 75)

Lenz then sets up a familiar literary model: the submission to divine judgement in a David and Goliath mould. A swimming race is to determine what is truth, and here, in contrast to the novels, Pilate is very clearly jesting. Again the unexpected happens; that is, the outcome is neither that which the relative strengths of the protagonists makes likely, nor that which the literary precedent of David and Goliath demands. The race is a draw, but if this is philosophically satisfying,

93

the judgement depends not on God, but on a piece of floating horse-dung which impels Kuckuck to swim faster.

The characters are rogues, not villains. Alec Puch and his three (natural) sons do indeed relieve fellow villagers of food and drink for an Easter feast, but those robbed become (predictably to the reader, if not to the family Puch) the guests at the feast. Alec, incidentally, is one of the many characters described as habitually barefoot, a motif which recurs in Lenz's other writings, seeming to denote simplicity and links with Nature, although it can elsewhere be sinister, as with the barefoot Mau-Mau terrorist Lukas in one of the short stories.

It is of interest to consider some literary antecedents of the Suleyken stories, which do not exist in an historical vacuum. Leaving aside the earlier forms of *Schwank* (medieval burlesque tales), we may refer to three literary traditions: that of the 'town of fools'; that of regional literature— 'Heimatsliteratur'; and that of the village tale, the 'Dorf-geschichte', in some senses a special aspect of the second tradition.

The 'town of fools' is the broadest of the three—Abdera or Chelm are examples, as are the sixteenth-century German Schildbürger[27] tales or the Wise Men of Gotham. The basic situation is a logical but foolish decision made by members of a town of fools. The men of Suleyken, however, are not fools in the same sense, in that they are not pretentious, as in some of the versions of the ramified fool tradition.

For the regional novel we may refer to J. P. Hebel in the eighteenth century, Peter Rosegger in the nineteenth and Ludwig Thoma in our own century. The degeneration of this type of writing into 'Blut-und-Boden-Literatur' (that is, literature of an overtly nationalistic character) led to its discrediting in the Nazi period, of course, but Lenz has in a sense revived it in a pure form, although he does mock the excesses of the tradition here and in the Bollerup stories—both the collections show self-irony which is fairly rare in Lenz's work. Worthy of close comparison here (and also in the context of Bollerup) is Fritz Reuter, the Low German writer of the nineteenth century, whose characters often anticipate Lenz's in their inventive reaction to life: Onkel Braesig of Reuter's tales is close in some ways to the many uncles claimed by Lenz in Suleyken, but Reuter is often sentimental, and Lenz never is.

For the *Dorfgeschichte*, parallels to Lenz in what might seem to be disparate writers may be noted. One, Sholem Aleichem, is perhaps less familiar to English readers, but his stories of life in the eastern European *shtetl* (the Yiddish word conveying still, it seems, overtones of endearment, as in the title to Lenz's stories) have much in common with Suleyken. Similar attitudes in a similar milieu are met with, and Lenz and Sholem Aleichem adopt similar narrative rôles. But Lenz's Suleyken is not shown as being under general physical threat.

Berthold Auerbach's Black Forest Village Tales, and more frequently Gottfried Keller's tales of the imaginary Swiss village of Seldwyla have been noted as part of the literary ancestry of Suleyken. Seldwyla's importance lies in its potential reality, rather than its actual position, and so too does Suleyken's. But where Suleyken is expressly hermetic, Seldwyla functions more as a yardstick: people come to and leave Seldwyla. Suleyken belongs already to history—perhaps to the 'backwaters of history', as Lenz himself tells us (Sul., p. 148) but it is sealed off in the past as well as in the Masurian lakes and marshes. Seldwyla has some connection with the outside world.

Critics have linked these stories, finally, with the writings of Jean Paul, the first writer to refer to Krähwinkel, the imaginary and proverbial backwoods village, and in the portrayal of humorous situations Jean Paul's style of intrusive narrator-irony anticipates Lenz. Jean Paul's tale of the 'Little Schoolmaster Maria Wutz' (and the *-chen* or *-lein* diminutives make translating Lenz's tales very difficult too) is referred to as *Eine Art Idylle* (A Sort of Idyll) and so too Lenz's book is an ironic idyll of childhood. The relationship

95

between reader, characters and narrator set up by Lenz may be seen already in Jean Paul's *Quintus Fixlein*. One example may suffice:

> The readers themselves will be all the more amused to hear, as they do now, that our Quintus has been invited to tea . . . by the local lord spiritual . . . and indeed, they will be as pleased as if they themselves had been invited.[28]

Much of the appeal of the collection lies in the style, and Lenz uses this particular tone frequently and couples it with an even more direct address:

> What shall I mention first? The dedication ceremony? Right. The dedication. This took place, as is well-known, on an innocent Spring day. (Sul., p. 86)

Sometimes, the narrator to reader relationship is still more direct:

> Right, then, and anyone who refuses to believe what happened next is advised to go and boil his head, but at least to stop reading now. (Sul., p. 137)

Other speech-gestures link the narrator with the characters, although some might be interpreted as having a distancing or disparaging effect, at least a patronising one. The frequent diminutives (a dialect feature) are ambiguous in this way. The characters use them—Zoppek calls the Prussian knights 'Ritterchen'—the concept is untranslatable, as indeed other phonological elements of the dialect are too. Narrator and characters alike employ dialect words or Polish elements, sometimes, but not always, translated. Most, though perhaps not all, would be familiar to a West German audience, though there may be an age barrier here. On the other hand, this is not the striving for linguistic realism that we encounter in Reuter. Lenz exploits the satirical device of an ironically elevated language used for subjects not normally associated with that language. An example from the narrator:

96

Hardly had the rumour arisen than it did what plainly lay in its nature: it spread itself. Spread itself all over Suleyken, leaped over to Schissomir, sprinted down the railway track until it got to Striegeldorf and arrived, this rumour, once it had crossed the Kulkarer meadows, right in the county town. Here it lost a little of its strength, having apparently taken a wrong turning, but eventually it got its bearings. It strutted across the market-place one day, marched up the steps to the council chambers, knocked at a certain door and there, as you might say, it was. (Sul., p. 108)

(Lenz uses similar devices without comic effect—and inappropriately—in his serious works too.) The people of Suleyken speak the same elevated ironic language, however, though not usually with such extended personification. Only a few taciturn types (where that taciturnity is the point of the story) fail to do so. Aunt Arafa, for example, arrives in Wszczinsk (we are solemnly assured that the name sounds beautiful in Polish) and demands a bath, but the great wooden bathtub is occupied by the village dotard. Although assured that he will have no objections to Aunt Arafa joining him, she demurs, and demands his removal. The innkeeper's reply is as courtly as Arafa's counter-arguments:

'No,' said the innkeeper. 'This desire to move Stanislaus Skrrbik to relinquish the bathtub voluntarily, even though it be for a brief period only, is unlikely to be fulfilled. He is far too attached to the tub. He would, as I know him, behave as if he had not grasped the nature of our demands.'

'In other words,' said Aunt Arafa, 'my right to a bath is being placed in question?' (Sul., p. 43)

Critics have raised the point that Lenz apparently wrote these tales to present a personalised picture of his childhood country to his wife. In general-critical terms, the fact is of dubious relevance. The stories do not tell us very much about Masuria, and some of the characteristics of the people would bear transplanting to other milieux. Nevertheless, Suleyken can have a general significance. The people of Suleyken can stand as representatives of a lost literalness and naivety that is no more because time has passed, or because civilisation has impinged itself more forcefully. This interpretation bids fair to outlast the idea of their providing a record of Masuria as such, the more so as the audience that can place the stories in a precise context is decreasing. It is a loss of Paradise as much as a loss of East Prussia. Lenz's other characters are forced by circumstances to reflect, and to consider problems. Hamilkar Schass can ignore the rifle of Wawrila. The central figures of *Es waren Habichte in der Luft* cannot. Hans Wagener has seen the stories as a 'utopian escape', and they have been linked with Heinrich Böll's pictures of Ireland in his *Irisches Tagebuch*.[29] They *are* escapist—the outcomes are always satisfactory,[30] honour or face are never lost: when the 'right-of-way duel' is broken up, we are even told that the crane swings both of the protagonists *forwards*. The aim is to entertain, and the stories do that admirably.

It is perhaps at least partly a result of the memory of the Suleyken tales that *Der Geist der Mirabelle* (Plum Spirit) enjoyed instant success on its publication in February 1975, running into a second impression of 50,000 copies a month later. While there may be elements here of a writer returning, perhaps for his own relaxation, to a proven formula, the comparison between these tales and the earlier group is less self-evident than it may at first appear. The topography is, of course, different: we are now in North Germany, in a town called Bollerup and Lenz tells us in a foreword that we are not in a lost idyllic golden age, but in the present, albeit still out in the country. Bollerup is closer to the outside world than was Suleyken, but it is not yet *in* it. Influences penetrate to Bollerup: reporters do arrive, where military men were actually repulsed from Suleyken. There is even a poetry reading in Bollerup. The parallel to Seldwyla is closer than it was with the earlier stories, for all that the actual milieu is that of Fritz Reuter or perhaps Theodor Storm. In social terms, Bollerup and Suleyken are comparable, with the regional difference that here we have fishermen as well as farmers. The narrator once again claims at least indirect relationship with the people—almost all surnamed Feddersen, but the linguistic individuality is less prominent. Some of the same narrative gestures are used. Here the direct narrative, punctuated with the apostrophising *Nachbarn* (neighbours), takes the place of the quasi-direct speech in the other tales. But now it has become stereotyped where before it was unforced, the narrator-objectivity is far greater, and the ironic courtliness is also missing. The people of Bollerup are not like children playing adult rôles in a complicated but logical game, and perhaps for this reason the stories have less of the immediately entertaining feel of the Masurian tales. Assertions of reality are made from time to time in the Bollerup stories, but children's phrases like *Ehrenwort*—word of honour—are missing. The nature of Bollerup is presumed to be verifiable, whereas Suleyken definitely belonged to the past.

So, too, the inhabitants sometimes resemble those of Masuria, but more frequently differ from them, and they are less uniform. In contrast to the barefoot Masurians, we have here a sort of halfway stage to civilisation. In Suleyken the people were protected even from moral charges by their patent innocence, but those in Bollerup can act with a devious forethought which, though it has some affinities with the child-logic of Suleyken, can be unpleasant. In Suleyken things usually worked out: the sufferers were, if anyone, the outsiders. In Bollerup, any folly receives its due punishment.

The stubbornness and stoicism, as well as the related attitude to time passing, are still there, and Bollerup is in some senses as timeless, or as little time-conscious as Suleyken, something essential to the *Schwank* as a genre. Sven Feddersen postpones his wedding for nine years in order to drink in solitary enjoyment the cellarful of blackcurrant wine that he has inherited. Merited blows of fate are accepted. When Franz Feddersen's wood-supply begins to disappear, he plants a powder-filled log, waits for the explosion and then goes to watch the culprit as he copes with the resulting fire. On hearing that the stove 'exploded because of its age' he makes the following comment: 'I've heard that that can happen, but I've also heard that some stoves only explode because a certain type of wood is unsuitable for them.' 'That might be it,' is the reply.'So in future I shall collect my wood a little further away.' (GdM., p. 67)

The outside world, though nearer, is sometimes viewed as a peril, just as it was in Suleyken. This is exemplified in the tale of the oldest inhabitant. Reporters come to interview the reputably super-active nonogenarian Birte Feddersen, and find her apparently senile and infirm. But they are suspicious, and—in Suleyken style—settle down to wait. It emerges that the old lady is indeed really hale, but was afraid that the reporters are officials come to take away her pension. And why is she so healthy? Whenever her husband had any serum left over from injecting the animals, he gave her the rest *hinterher*—does this only mean afterwards in a time sense? (GdM., p. 108 f). The Plock children in Suleyken suffered after genuine inoculation, and Birte lives to a ripe age on animal serum.

Equally predictable is the final tale here, of a taciturn woodsman picked as a 'favourite son', but essentially silent candidate by a political party, who makes a grass-roots speech of his own before prudently withdrawing, and thus preserving his integrity. He is the 'secret winner' of the election, and it is irrelevant which of the otherwise indistinguishable parties actually wins.

In Suleyken, the characters may quarrel from time to time, but the quarrels are always sorted out. However, this is not true in Bollerup. An apparent reconciliation in time of adversity between two men whose families have feuded (for reasons now forgotten) for years is only illusory. The trouble of the moment forgotten, the feud goes on.

An example of the deviousness which replaces the innocent instinct of Suleyken is provided by the tale of the *Hausschlachtung* (Home-Cured Pig). Unwilling to pay the local slaughterer, Uwe Feddersen determines to persuade the most villainous-looking of the local convicts on work detail to escape and kill the pig for him. To this end his wife puts in considerable effort (including going to bed with the convict), but it transpires that although the man may look villainous, he is in reality a squeamish, though skilled burglar, who absconds with some of the Feddersen's property. The devotion to the plan, itself based on greed, has all the trappings of the late medieval *Schwank*, the foolish peasant who *deserves* to be robbed and cuckolded. The ancestors of this tale are Hans Sachs and Boccaccio, not the absurdly logical people of Sulyken.

Worthy of special consideration, too, is the story of the Bollerup poetry-reading given by the local regional poetess,[31] Alma Bruhm-Feddersen, an occasion as unique as the visit of the circus to Suleyken, and comparable with it. Many of the lady's poems derive from Eichendorff or Goethe—'Erlkönig' (The Erl King) is turned into a tale of a veterinary surgeon on his way, presumably, to a sick animal—and some of the external humour depends on this, as a literary joke. The local people do not recognise this anyway, but they do insist on the very literal correction of 'errors' in the poems. The consciously literary atmosphere is rather different from that of the circus. So too, the titles of the Bollerup stories are deliberately literary: a title like 'Die Bauerndichterin' (The Regional Poetess) may be assumed to arouse some expectations in the reader, since it is a known literary concept. The Suleyken tales, on the other hand have as their primary heading 'The First of the Masurian Stories' and so on, giving at once the idea of a book for children, and of a closed group.

Some of the elements here are almost too familiar. Wagener rightly draws attention to the antiquity of the plot in 'An Expensive Joke' (doctor is called out at night to attend to a broken leg—the leg is that of a table, but he gets revenge when he presents his bill).[32] Some of the jokes in the Suleyken series were also predictable, but it is perhaps a mistake to link the story-cycles too closely, as Walther Killy, for example, has done:

Beside his problematic productions, Lenz has, out of just polite-
ness, set, one feels, two works of unproblematical roguery, in
which the reader may seek recuperation . . . In [*Suleyken and
Bollerup*] everything is on the surface, funny or a little grotesque,
these are wood-cut-style jokes that are dependable, just like the
people of the lost Masurian world, just like the inhabitants of
Bollerup. There the relationships are always clear, sometimes
crafty, but the hearts are always in the right place . . . No longer
is the past a fleeting phantom, but is sunlit, a friendly light shines
on the coasts.[33]

The cycles are not the same. The sun shone all the time in the
childhood of Suleyken. In Bollerup it sometimes rains,
although not as often as it does in real life.

7

THE SHORT STORIES—II

In addition to the tales of Suleyken and Bollerup, fifty other
stories by Lenz have been collected in four books, and a
good many are still uncollected. In view of this, we can
concentrate here only upon the stories in those four collections: *Jäger des Spotts* (Hunter of Mockery, 1958), *Das Feuerschiff* (The Lightship, 1960), *Der Spielverderber* (The Spoilsport, 1964) and *Einstein überquert die Elbe Bei Hamburg* (Einstein crosses the Elbe at Hamburg, 1975). The first three
volumes were collected in one volume, *Gesammelte
Erzählungen*, in 1970. Each of the collections takes its title
from a story in the collection, but the relationship to the
whole can differ. The story 'Jäger des Spotts' does indeed
set a Hemingway-esque tone for many, but not all, of those
in the collection. *Das Feuerschiff*, however, is simply the
dominant story, the length of a novella, and has been
treated as such already in an earlier chapter. It has been
translated, although translations of the short stories are
otherwise fairly rare. *Der Spielverderber* takes its title from the
most important story of the collection, but the last collection seems to be entitled from the most experimental of a
stylistically far more varied collection, and one with less
unity than the earlier groups. We must add here, finally, a
collection of linked stories, almost a brief episodic novel, the
amusing but not very deep *Lehmann's Erzählungen*, the tales
of Lehmann, a black marketeer, published in 1964.

Lenz has noted dates of origin for the stories, but this
occasionally presents problems. Thus he gives 1950 as the
date of inception of the title story of *Jäger des Spotts*. Its close
proximity to Hemingway's *The Old Man and the Sea* (which

appeared in 1952) seems to indicate that it was at least remoulded before publication.

Lenz has defended the short story in an essay 'Gnadengesuch für die Geshichte' (Plea for Mercy for the Short Story), in which he notes as the ingredients:

> Imagination, necessary considerations, careful structure, the elimination of coincidence, proper connexions. (Bez., p. 95)

and the discipline of the story attracts him. He is aware of the basic stylistic essentials: that it must be short and that there must be a story. Beyond this it is notoriously difficult to go. If we extend the length, we arrive at the novella, with its extra demands upon narrative concentration and singleness of plot. Kurt Kusenberg's interesting essay on the short story looks for a 'paradoxical change in events', a narrative of the unexpected, and 'man's impotence in the face of fate'. These comments could apply to most German novellas, to Lenz's short stories as indeed to Aeschylus' drama, and a severely pragmatic definition is required: a narrative of unusual interest, brief and therefore probably concentrated on a limited range of characters or themes, told nowadays usually in prose (although this was not always the case).[34]

Lenz's themes can be categorised to a certain extent. We may make a division to begin with between satire and the serious short story, and place in the first category *Lehmanns Erzählungen* and a few tales strongly influenced by Böll. The themes of family strife, death, even murder, plainly come within the other category, although there *is* sometimes an overlap. The mention of satire, however, gives the clue to Lenz's overriding theme—the conflict between how things look and how they actually are, which is very frequently a reflection of man's desire to go against fate coupled with his patent inability to do so. Within this framework, Lenz explores several themes: family relationships, especially marital ones; the relationship to the past and the reaction to the new political and social situation after the great divide of the war; and the theme of the novels—man trying fate and failing, due to some sort of inevitability, such as age.

Some features are common to all the short stories, and one of them is the ability to remember that a story must entertain. Lenz is capable of tension, and of holding interest. This is not to say that the stories always succeed, once the end has been reached and the point or twist made, but in the telling is much of value—and this is vital for any storyteller.

Lenz varies his point of view, although he uses most frequently the first-person narrator, usually the central figure, but sometimes an observer, more objective than involved, and rarely commenting on the events. Sometimes, however, this technique appears to be used for its own sake, and adds little, becoming more a simple literary affectation.[35] Even objective narratives may be made more real by the adoption of a collective identity—a 'we' voice. In the most recent volume, there are experimental pieces—with varying voices for the same story, or with straightforward or thinly veiled dialogue, and Lenz has used too the dramatic monologue, where the other voices are implied.

In the earliest collections the influence of Böll on the satires and Hemingway on the serious stories is apparent. How far Lenz has developed is evident in the title story of the most recent collection, which has its own subtitle 'Story in three Sentences', although Hemingway's directness is still encountered.

There are other constants: these include the setting for many of the stories, the North German coast, which Lenz is able to evoke particularly well, as he does in *Deutschstunde*—and here more than anywhere, Lenz's prose recalls the paratactic Low German of Fritz Reuter a century earlier. The special setting, echoing Reuter and sometimes the mood, though not the style, of Theodor Storm, recurs in several stories.

Individual symbols also recur: the optical visualisation of scenes, through a telescope or field-glasses, are often linked with the coast-tales. Photographs, too, play a part, and Lenz is fond of elemental imagery (or of the pathetic fallacy), as the title of 'Stimmungen der See' (Moods of the Sea) indicates. The sea becomes real, a force, rarely of sexuality, but often of fatal inexorability. In the satires, Lenz is fond of multiple irony at the end of a story, leading the reader to expect one point, bringing him to another, and then sometimes taking yet another turn, an ironic reversal.

Much of the criticism of Lenz's stories—at least, of the earlier ones—has been dominated by comparisons with Hemingway, and this is due by and large to an essay in which Lenz acknowledges his debt to, and talks about, his ultimate break away from his American model.[36] The American writer may well have interested Lenz on several levels. Hemingway was himself very aware of his failing faculties,[37] and the loss of power through the onset of age is a typical Lenz theme. What Lenz took from him for the first short stories was partly thematic—sportsmen (though they are runners, and not bullfighters), word-shy tough men, and men facing an existential moment of truth. No that they all need to be tough—Francis Macomber, in one of Hemingway's better stories, is not, and indeed, Lenz's heroes rarely have the total toughness of, say, Harry Morgan in *To Have and Have Not*. Lenz's work contains too even fewer erotic elements than Hemingway's. Eventually, Lenz tells us, he moved away from the idea of one existential moment, in favour of a represented continuum, but the influence on the early stories is clear. Lenz tells us that he broke with Hemingway thematically with a story in *Das Feuerschiff* called 'Der Anfang von Etwas' (The Beginning of Something), where he wanted to write a beginning rather than the end implied in the Hemingway story, 'The End of Something'. The argument is not entirely convincing, and indeed the style lasts beyond the collection involved.

There have been other influences, mainly figures from American literature, and Lenz has written about Faulkner, for example. Closer to home is the patent influence of Böll, and Borchert has been acknowledged. Lenz has been a member of the German literary circle, *Gruppe 47*, and has followed in his own development the move from *Kahlschlag-Prosa* (bare writing) to stylistic experimentation.[38]

The major collections include relatively few satires, but the separate volume *Lehmanns Erzählungen, oder So schön war mein Markt* (Lehmann's Tales, or Oh What a Lovely Market, 1964), may be included under this heading. The second title of the work echoes that of the highly popular Suleyken tales, and there are points of similarity. The sub-title, *Aus den Bekenntnissen eines Schwarzhändlers* (From the Memoirs of a Black-Marketeer) is modelled presumably on that of Thomas Mann's *Felix Krull*, and again there are similarities. Lenz's six anecdotes show us episodes in the picaresque post-war life of the black marketeer Lehmann, crooked, but unlike most of Lenz's characters, inevitably a winner, a man endowed with the wit and the imagination of the characters in the Suleyken stories. Lehmann embarks on his career because he finds himself, at the end of the war, with a supply of coffee spoons and little else. But there is a shortage of these, however necessary or unnecessary these may in fact be, and on them he builds his empire, going on to bigger and better deals and comforts. He supplies the Allies with first-rate liquor (preserving alcohol, with most of the preserved specimens removed, at least), transports illegal silver with the help of a baby in a bathtub, shifts off-ration meat in a series of regular funerals, and even makes life in prison (his stay is very short) most comfortable. His masterpiece is in the fourth tale, where he is able to supply a monument to gratify the whim of an old man, whose relatives are willing to pay in commodities of greater use. Lehmann provides a massive statue of the Great Elector, once standing in East Prussia, and reprieved from the melting-down that is the fate of statues of warriors in spiked helmets because he is dressed (more or less) as a huntsman. The ironic twist is that the man who ordered the statue for his father's delectation realises at once that this monument is from his own home town, and that his aged father contributed towards its erection. Lenz twists the conclusion several times, in a very small space, with considerable comic effect. The last twist may be cited—the old man is in fact delighted with the massive reminder of home, even if his younger relatives are not, and 'he had a bench put up beneath it, and often sat there until he caught pneumonia and died.' (Leh., p. 86). The comedy avoids predictability, leaving us with good entertainment, but it is fair to ask whether there is any more to it than this neat use of the eternal popularity of the picaresque, set in a world that is gone, but not entirely forgotten. Are these stories really satires, the term implying a corrective in morals or manners to some degree at least?

There are incidents which are capable of interpretation as a comment on the times—the re-erection of the Great Elector is perhaps one of them. But the entertainment predominates, and one hopes that it has made money, a function that should not be ignored by the critics when trying to evaluate the popularity of a writer. For all that, there *is* an overall satirical point. The stories were published in 1964, at a time of great prosperity, and perhaps there is even an element in its popularity (sales had reached 125,000 by 1975) of nostalgia for the bad times seen through the rose-tinted spectacles of prosperity. There may also be a memorial function; Lehmann, the first-person narrator, tells us at the very beginning that he belongs to the past—the currency reform of 1948 saw to that:

Since then I have been waiting, hoping that my moment of glory might come back—it hasn't done so yet. I find solace in my memories. Memory is the one thing that keeps me alert and sprightly, but since even memory—I can feel it—gets blurred, like old photographs, I want to write it all down, for the benefit of the like-minded. (Leh., p. 10)

In a time of prosperity, then, a reminder that there are Lehmanns around, who, however lovable, are still crooks, and they will return in times of scarcity. But this is the only indication of the serious side, and the book stands as a comic piece, successfully treated, with the narrator seeing himself as a Walt Whitman (at least, wishing he were), singing not of himself but of the Black Market and the Art of Scarcity—and is not economics defined as the 'science of scarcity'?

The satirical writings of Heinrich Böll set the tone of many of Lenz's other satires, however, as well as showing similar themes. The most noticeable stylistic element is the use of elegant and allusive language in describing what is in reality unpleasant. Some of Lenz's stories are very close indeed to Böll—and of 'Die Lampen der Eskimos' (Lamps of the Eskimos, 1959 Sv.). W. L. Schwarz has said:

> The most significant difference from Böll's Rujuk-story ('Im Lande der Rujuks', 1953) seems to be that Böll's native tribesmen are from the South Seas, and Lenz's Eskimos are from Greenland.[39]

and several of the others can be linked with Böll stories, 'Mein verdrossenes Gesicht' (My Miserable Face, in JdS. but dated from 1950 by Lenz) echoes 'Mein trauriges Gesicht' by Böll (1950), 'Der Grosse Wildenberg' (The Great Wildenberg, 1954 JdS.) has much in common with 'Es wird etwas geschehen' (1954), 'Der Amüsierdoktor' (PhD in Entertainment, 1960 Fs.) links with 'Der Lacher' (1952) or even Böll's 'Dr Murke' (1955) in the futility of the occupation involved, and the general contrast between occupation and private life in 'Der seelische Ratgeber (Spiritual Counsellor, 1959 JdS.) can be seen in several of Böll's stories.[40]

Lenz is, however, far more of an overt moralist than Böll, who presents his absurd characters, and may at best leave them thinking about their positions. Lenz's satires are more frequently rounded off, and as such are more serious in intent, and the distinction from the serious story is often tenuous—the tale 'Ein Haus aus lauter Liebe' (House of Pure Love, 1952 JdS.) is a case in point. The idea of overcoming the past appears in serious and satirical stories alike. 'Der Spielverderber' (The Spoilsport, 1962) has as a central character a destitute, living in a sort of shanty-town, with the unnerving ability to 'recall' conveniently forgotten facts about the past. Thus he sees a clock in the house of his teacher, and involuntarily comes up with the name of its last owner—a Jew. This forces the narrator out of society, but he can be a symbol of the post-war writer, reminding his fellows of the past, serving as a conscience. The same theme is found in 'Nachzahlung' (Back Pay, 1964 Sv.), a first person narrative from the point of view of an involved bystander. Josef Tubacki, a junk dealer, goes back to a factory in which he was a forced-labourer during the war, to claim the DM 29.80 still owing to him in wages. The management is hugely embarrassed, and offers him large sums. Tubacki refuses this, and eventually the management, playing according to his stubborn rules, work out that with insurance contributions and so on, Tubacki owes *them* money. 'Mein verdrossenes Gesicht' is also to do with the war in a sense, although it also forms a bridge to the new society. The central figure, with a face permanently soured by the war, encounters a former comrade who, like the others, has come to terms with the new society. His sour face gets the narrator a job as the 'envious onlooker' in advertisements, a job which he loses—and this is the characteristic Lenz twist—when his sour expression is replaced by one of real sympathy.

Two other tales might be placed in the category of satire, although they perhaps do not fulfil the equally important criterion that they must be humorous as well as serious. 'Lieblingsspeise der Hyänen' (Favourite Food for Hyenas, 1969 Fs.) deals with an American visiting Europe with a view to making good some of the experiences of the war (apologising to an Italian shepherd whose sheep he killed on a bridge he had to bomb, or visiting the grave of a dead comrade). His aims are thwarted because his wife and daughter spend all their time buying shoes. The American—although he shows some kind of resolve to break away, in fact does not do so—he allows his women to manipulate him, and the honourable intentions are subjected to the pursuit of the material world. The absurdity of the shoe-purchasing perhaps makes this a satire, but the tale is really a serious one, and recalls *Duell mit dem Schatten* in some respects. Similar is 'Die Strafe' (Punishment, 1970 Ein.), the only tale even to approach satire in the most recent of the collections. Here an old man is constantly producing evidence to have himself tried for his share of collective war-time guilt—but always without success: even a mock trial fails to satisfy him.

Three satires touch on aspects of the new Germany, in the spirit of criticism associated with the *Gruppe 47*: 'Der Amüsierdoktor', 'Der Grosse Wildenberg' and 'Die Lampen der Eskimos', all of these, as has been noted, are closely connected with Böll's satires, and in a way bound, as are Böll's tales, to their chronological point of reference. The two latter stories, moreover, could almost be by Böll: Wildenberg is a factory tycoon, shielded from all comers—including the narrator—by countless members of staff (Lenz uses the same theme in 'Nachzahlung'). When finally reached by the narrator, he turns out to be a pathetic and lonely figure quite unable to deal with the narrator's request, but eager that he should return and keep him company again. We never establish what the factory produces. 'Die Lampen der Eskimos' is told by the leader of an institute specialising in a minimal area of folklore—Eskimo lamps from one part of Greenland. Huge subsidies are spent on obtaining material for the production of equally huge scholarly treatises. When the director visits the supplier, he finds a sophisticated and ultra-modern production-line, where lamps are specially made and appropriately dented and damaged. The point is exactly that of Böll's Rujuk-story, where the student of the language arrives in the land of the Rujuks to find them completely Americanised. Time has gone too fast for the scholar in Böll's story, in Lenz's the director is the victim of a simple confidence trick. However, Böll's narrator gives up, keeping the pretence of interest only for his professor, who is still in ignorance of the situation; Lenz's narrator decides to carry on, seemingly bitter at what he has discovered. But is he? The subsidies have been raised, and 'perhaps in the latest

111

consignment there is something of interest.' (Sv., p. 61) The onset of deliberate cynicism or studied ignorance ends the tale.

Only 'Der Amüsierdoktor' is quite different, although his general futility has much in common with Böll's 'Dr Murke'. Lenz's character has the job of amusing customers in a factory and we meet the character, in fact, in *Brot und Spiele*, where he plays a serious part and indeed suffers an accident at the mammoth fish-shredding machine (which is named Robespierre). The machine plays a part here too, but there is an interesting twist, and the tale is not tragic—though it might have been: forced with the task of amusing an apparently un-amusable Aleutian Islander, the Doctor of Entertainment seems to have met his match—not even the usual round of strippers, and a nicely ludicrous 'Judgement of Paris' parody (which owes a little to Böll's 'Es wird etwas geschehen' in which a super-secretary moonlights as 'Vamp 7') can move him to delight. Only when the Doctor climbs into the fish-shredder and comes near to being chopped up does the *Naturmensch* (noble savage) laugh. The Doctor has succeeded, but the cost to his dignity and nearly his life make the point very clear.

Two further tales come close to being serious, and demonstrate satire only in a basically ludicrous situation: 'Die Glücksfamilie des Monats' (This Month's Lucky Family, 1964 Sv.) and 'Der seelische Ratgeber' are both concerned with newspapers. The second owes a little to Nathanael West's *Miss Lonelyhearts* in showing us the dichotomy between appearance and reality in the person of an agony columnist, dispensing sweetness and light whilst subsisting on gin. His assistant, the narrator, becomes gradually disillusioned when, having been sent on errands to members of the columnist's family, he discovers that the man's private life is in chaos, and his own wife and children have nothing but scorn for him. The story is not especially successful, lacking the breadth of, say *Miss Lonelyhearts,* and it is too easy for it to imply sympathy for the columnist, since we do not know, for example, why his children are against him. The narrator learns something about human nature, perhaps, but initially he is pretty naive. The first story is better drawn, and Lenz manages a twist at the end which lends irony to the title. A caretaker at a school, formerly a teacher, but unable to speak properly, lives with his wife and son (who is the narrator) as an object of mockery because of his impediment. But a newspaper selects them at random as 'the month's lucky family', offering them outings, which will be heavily publicised. The reporter and the attendant photographer are very well portrayed and Lenz is able to sketch their total lack of concern with this family very neatly indeed. The outings are disastrous: the father, attempting to make a speech at a meeting, is laughed at because of his defect, and he is hit by a jib and injured at the last outing. The accident, though, has deprived the man of his powers of speech altogether, and 'if he can't speak, then they will leave him in peace.' (Sv., p.98). The irony is double, and the story is satirical only in certain elements of style and some of the motifs.

One other story deserves comment here: 'Der Sohn des Diktators' (The Son of the Dictator, 1960 Fs.) is the first-person account of how a son, now in prison, had tried to take over from his father, dictator of an unspecified Eastern European country (the names look faintly Hungarian). The son's carefully planned attempts to have the father blown up come to naught, as the father has been following his plots, and has arranged instead the 'heroic death' of the son himself (or rather his double), ostensibly whilst saving the father's life. The tale is a cynical comment on political villainy, or even on human nature—the son's co-plotters give things away because they have been given positions, but not hard cash. The son has a lot to learn. The setting of the story, however Ruritanian, nevertheless points to the East, and this is true too of a serious tale 'Ein Freund der Regierung' (A Friend of the Government, 1959) included in the same volume, and very much a counter to this one.

Summarising the satires: stylistically, all are first-person narratives, told at least by persons involved with the main characters, and this and the tone cannot but call Böll to mind. A general difference is there, however, in the question of *how* the moral is drawn. Böll's characters exist for themselves (and Lenz's essay on Böll makes clear the former's admiration of just this aspect of the latter's work). This is sometimes the case with Lenz's figures—the agony columnist is as much a simple representation of a *Schein/Sein* dichotomy (gulf between being and seeming) as the dogcatcher in one of Böll's tales who keeps an unlicensed dog. But the twists at the end of 'Der Amüsierdoktor' or the 'Glücksfamilie' show a difference of tone, almost as if Lenz is not entirely happy with pure satire, and contrasting with, say, 'Der grosse Wildenberg' or 'Die Lampen der Eskimos' which are, in all conscience, little more than Böll imitations. The more serious themes developed in tales like 'Der Spielverderber', however, seem to betoken (as happened with Hemingway) a move from a specific influence on a young man. The most successful of the satires, those combining amusement with a point intended to ameliorate through accentuation some aspect of human manners, come in the third collection—*Der Spielverderber*. The most recent collection contains very little in this vein, and the Lehmann stories may be considered as having primarily an entertainment value, whatever else may be read into them. This is not, incidentally, meant pejoratively; that they are very well done is surely sufficient.

The serious stories far outnumber the satires, but the themes are similar; war and the past; the new Germany and the new political situation in the world; personal relationships, especially within families; and human failure. The influence of Böll satires does, in fact, continue, and echoes of Böll's 'Nicht nur zur Weihnachtszeit' (Not just at Christmas)—or even of Borchert's stories—may be felt in Lenz's focus upon festivals—often New Year.

The serious stories provide, of course, more opportunity for experiment, and we find in the three earlier collections a

114

mixture of directly and indirectly involved first-person narrative, objective story-telling, and—in the fourth collection—experiments with point of view, with objective framework and varied inner viewpoints, with different narrators, and with a cross-over from prose dialogue to the techniques of the radio play. 'Herr und Frau S. in Erwartung ihrer Gäste' (Mr and Mrs S. Waiting for their Guests, 1973 Ein.) and 'Die Augenbinde' (The Blindfold, 1966 Ein.) are cases in point. The first, though in a collection of short stories, is clearly a drama, and other works are one-sided dialogues: 'Ball der Wohltäter' (Benefit Ball, 1959 Sv.), '18 Diapositive' (18 Colour-Slides, 1973 Ein.); *Die Augenbinde* has been presented as a radio play in its own right, but the theme is treated as a short story with a dominant narrator.

Lenz has, like other writers, been preoccupied from the beginnings of his short story publications too with the problem of *Vergangenheitsbewältigung*, coming to terms with the past. A few stories are, indeed, actually set in the war, and derive their effect from the conflict between the major event and the individual. An important example is 'Gelegenheit zum Verzicht', a story later given the title 'Der Verzicht' ([Opportunity for] Resignation *or* Objection, 1960 Sv.) which, as Walter Schmähling has indicated,[41] makes its point by the uncommented isolation of an incident concerned with the extermination of the Jews. The horrors of that aspect of the Nazi epoch are too great to be grasped, and it is of course generally accepted that a massive figure—like 'six million'—can at best have only an emblematic effect, whereas the reality and individuality of Anne Frank probably still bring the atrocities home far more clearly and memorably. Anne Frank was of course real, and Heilmann in this story is not, but the place is: we are in Masuria once again, but in a context entirely different from that of Suleyken.

The story is very simple. The last Jew in the area has to be arrested by the elderly and ailing instrument of Nazi power in the village, the policeman, Bielek. The story demonstrates

115

that the Nazi atrocities reached down to every level, and in a
sense the plot is that of *Deutschstunde*. Bielek, like Ole Jepsen,
represents the duty-bound single-mindedness of the régime
incarnate in one old man in a village, where the objects of his
duty are personally known to him. One of Hitler's primary
attacks on the Jews was concerned with their economic
power. Heilmann runs a scrap-metal yard, from which children steal oddments and resell them to him for pennies. Nazi
Germany and Jewish economic power—in reality reduced to
two men as well-known to each other as Jepsen and Nansen,
neither of them filling the stereotypes, but resigned to their
rôles. A schoolboy warns Heilmann, who refuses, however,
to flee: there is no point. In the icy landscape, where could he
flee, and flight, too, would be an admission that he is somehow guilty.

The two men communicate very little, as indeed the boy
had not communicated with Heilmann in words. Everyone
knows what is going on:

'Ready Wilhelm?' 'Ready Heinrich'. It did not occur to Wilhelm
Heilmann to say anything more. (Sv., p. 27)

The few further exchanges are ironic: 'Not the friendliest of
days,' says Bielek. 'It'll be more pleasant in the forest' is the
answer. The rest is silence, as they make their way painfully
through the woods to Korczymmen, to the border. Heilmann
is delivered up, and we see forced labour and hear machine-
gunning; a younger man sends Bielek back, and then notices
that Heilmann has already walked ahead towards his fate.
He had expected the summons, had reckoned with it, and
'not once had he permitted himself the weakness of hope'
(Sv., p. 27). The story is impressive in its simplicity, and the
setting underlines the fact that these two old men are the
very end of the chain of conflict, in a symbolic sense, as well
as the fact that Heilmann is the last Jew in a world that is
frozen and inhospitable, but with icy grooves of inevitability; the first scene has been commented upon, but is
important:

116

In the middle of that winter he turned up with his bicycle and his mission, cycling in a frozen sled-track which did not allow him to raise his head and look forwards, but which forced him to follow inevitably the track which he had chosen for himself, always watching it, since when he looked up, the wheel-rim hit the ice-covered walls of snow, scraped along the handlebars twisted sideways, and when he turned them against this, the front wheel jammed sideways in the narrow groove, so that he had trouble . . . jumping off in time. (Sv., p. 23)

Bielek does not jump off.

The story is told objectively, but it is observed by a group of which Lenz is a member, and Heilmann is the last Jew in 'our hopeless corner of Masuria' (Sv., p. 26). The lack of hope combined with the lack of fear, and the uncommented presentation of an incident that brings the evil forces of the world even to the furthest corner of Masuria, needs no extra comment. The story is not exciting in the sense of some of Lenz's tales. There is no tension—although Bielek takes a certain time to realise this—that Heilmann will not escape. That there are virtually no spoken words makes the story the more powerful.

Only the reference to 'that Winter' in 'Der Verzicht' indicates the chronological distance between the narrator and the event. The distance from the war in time, but its real proximity nevertheless, is clearer in other stories. 'Lieblingsspeise der Hyänen' and 'Die Strafe' both refer back to the war but comment essentially upon the present. 'Schwierige Trauer' (Difficult Mourning—either difficult 'to bear' or 'to feel'—1960 Sv.) falls between the two, placing the narrative point of view firmly in the present, the events discussed in the past. Here there is a fuller narrator involvement, in that the story forms a funeral oration for Henry Smolka (the point of whose forename is problematic) given by his son. Again *Deutschstunde* comes to mind, for Smolka had insisted on duty above all else, to the detriment of lives. Charged at the end of the war—as the last mayor of Luknow, a town in East Prussia—with the task of

117

removing all official documents for safekeeping, he does this by requisitioning transport that could have been used for the sick, for refugees, even for his own daughter. Smolka loses most of the material on the way, and dies in a doss-house, still clutching the now useless fragments of the archives, which are buried with him.

The story is also directed at the present. The narrator refers to the possibility of Germany reclaiming these lands as 'absurd'—the father's archive material is 'absurd luggage, supposed to be used some time in support of an absurd claim.' (Sv., p. 127) The story becomes an acceptance and a plea for humanity, made effective by its directness: it is, after all, a speech.

Three other stories look more clearly to the war. One, 'Risiko für Weihnachtsmänner' (Father Christmases at Risk, 1958 Fs.), comes close to the grotesque. A hired Father Christmas is sent to the house of his former colonel. The soldier has lost his nose in the freezing snow when wounded on the Eastern Front, and his colonel visualises him and a remembered dead colleague as a dead Father Christmas. In his new rôle, the soldier is unable to make the threatening gestures traditionally made by Father Christmas in Germany to make sure the children have been good, and the whole becomes a comment on the war as such. Two stories from the most recent collection are at a further remove from the war. 'Herr und Frau S. in Erwartung ihrer Gäste' harks back to an individual incident, a private guilty past linked closely with, and using a motif from *Duell mit dem Schatten*. Mr and Mrs S. (who are given unexplained English forenames) have invited to dinner guests unbeknown to the other partner. Waiting for them, they lose their resolve not to reveal who these are. The husband tells about a certain Julius Gassmann, who was torpedoed, but was rescued wearing another man's jacket, and who, as a POW in America, simply adopted the other man's identity—the identity of the husband. The wife realises, and we see, that Julius Gassmann is already there:

118

No, Ann. It was your idea . . . the iceberg . . . the unknown
part . . . I tried and tried . . . there are no strangers to you that I
could have invited . . . only Julius Gassmann . . . And that is
me . . . I was him. (Ein., p. 165)

For the wife the whole relationship alters. The motif of the
switched jacket is developed in a different way—another
example of Lenz's interest in perspectives—and the implications of guilt are left for the reader to ponder. The war is
echoed too in '18 Diapositive': here not even as a direct
memory, but second-hand, evoked by photographs taken on
a *recent* holiday in England, of places that were important
during the time of emigration and which recall incidents
involving (but on different sides) the speaker and the guest to
whom he is showing the slides, now his boss. For the latter
the pictures produce only guilt.

The style of the two stories bears consideration. The first is
really a radio play, and even includes sound effects, like the
sudden false-alarm of a telephone. The second is a monologue, in which the pointed comments are interspersed with
day-to-day pleasantries. We are given the reaction of the
guests, although we neither see nor hear them, only gather
their state of mind from the comments of the speaker. Only
rarely does the irony of the situation become heavy:

I'm sorry Thea, but I don't understand why you are getting so
worked up . . .we're only looking at a few slides . . . Come on,
how can you say that anyone is being accused . . . There were two
sides, that's all. It was Eugen's fate to be on one side, and mine to
be on the other. (Ein., p. 225)

The guests made the choice to be on the 'other side' of an
historical situation which has, for example, forced a Jewish
historian to disguise himself as a guide in the Tower of
London, to enable him to link medieval cruelties with Nazi
Germany. However long ago, there is still room for guilt. The
story is a counter to 'Die Strafe', although the person who
should feel guilty in this case never speaks.

Serious stories on the problems of the new Germany are

119

rare. 'Wie bei Gogol' (Like a Story by Gogol, 1973 Ein.) is the story of a Turkish *Gastarbeiter* (immigrant worker) who wishes to remain anonymous (to the authorities) at all costs, even when genuine interest is being shown in him. The position of the immigrant worker is well-drawn, seen through the eyes of a modern German. 'Die Wellen der Balaton' (Waves at Lake Balaton, 1973 Ein.) shows objectively a failed reunion between members of a family now living in East and West Germany respectively: they are just too far apart, and not even some chance acquaintances from the West that appear first of all as interlopers, and have to be got rid of rather rudely, can be blamed. The complete difference of the two sides is underlined, although the East Germans leave to see the last (free) wild horses of the Puszta.

'Ein Freund der Regierung' is a political allegory. We are again in Eastern Europe, the names are Hungarian- (Bela) or Slav-looking (Garek). The title is ironic, and this kind of irony is perhaps now too commonplace: the reader of any post-war German story will expect this to be concerned with someone who is *not* a friend of the government, and one suspects that Lenz knows this, preempting superficial suspense (as in *Stadtgespräch*) in favour of developmental interest. Visiting journalists to this unnamed country are introduced to the pro-government Bela, who, they notice, has some teeth missing. His pronouncements on the state of the country are positive, even when the guide is absent, and even though we know that his son has been tortured for resistance to the régime. When the narrator shakes hands with him on leaving, however, a tooth is pressed into his hand—this is the entire point, and again there is no further comment, nor is any needed. Lenz returns to this aspect of the modern political scene in 'Die Schmerzen sind zumutbar' (The Level of Pain is Acceptable, 1966 Ein.). A major politician, to answer foreign criticism, wishes to show that his interrogation methods are not inhuman, by subjecting himself to them. We see him undergoing and accepting all the tortures, and, for the last, he is told that, 'like everyone else', he can raise his index finger if the pain is too great. He is surprised when the medical orderly appears at the end with splints and bandages—the prisoners usually have their index finger broken first.

Another group of stories may be given the overall heading of 'studies in relationships', and a favourite theme is tension between husband and wife. A small observational study 'Das Examen' (The Exam, 1969 Ein.) shows a wife preparing a small celebration for her husband's successful doctoral examination, but she is too ill to take part in the celebration after all. At the other end of the scale comes 'Die Flut ist pünktlich' (The Tide Comes on Time, 1953 JdS.) in which a woman has altered the time on her husband's watch so that he will be cut off by the tide and drowned. Her lover, with her, realises only gradually that this is what she is capable of. The setting of North German islands and mud-flats, which play such a part in much of Lenz's writing, can lend sombre atmosphere to similar tales. Thus the fairly recent 'Fallgesetze' (Laws of Gravity, 1973 Ein.) shows, from different points of view, a fake drowning in a marital triangle, and 'Küste im Fernglas' (The Coast through a Telescope, 1958 Sv.) seems to be an earlier version of the same theme through the eyes—and indeed through the restricted vision of the telescope—of the betrayed husband.

Marital breakdown that is not visible to the outside world forms the theme of other stories: 'How it is and how it seems' (the title of a not particularly illuminating article by E. N. Elstun) sums up several such stories. In 'Ein Haus aus lauter Liebe' a student takes a babysitting job at the home of a rich business man, who seems desperately concerned about his children, and indeed even comes back early. But the house is not one 'of pure love' at all. The man's wife, an actress and beauty, is presented fairly harshly, and during the evening a 'phone-call comes from someone who is patently her lover. The house has other secrets too. The father 'hasn't the heart to leave the children alone in the house' (JdS., p. 37) but keeps out of sight his old father, a former seaman, who joins

121

the student and drinks a considerable amount, but when the father returns has himself locked back in his room. The business man is, presumably, ashamed of his own father. The student observes all, and comments only 'yes, they were all good' (JdS., p. 44).

Other family situations are told objectively. In 'Der längere Arm' (The Longer Arm, 1959 Fs.) a wife realises that her husband is a blackmailer and destroys the means with which he exercises this power. 'Der Anfang von etwas' (The Beginning of Something, 1958 Fs.) shows a marriage which has broken down; but the husband takes advantage of the fact that he is supposed to have been on board a ship that is wrecked in order to adopt a new identity. While the story was supposedly intended as a kind of positive counter to Hemingway's 'End of Something', it is fair to say that a neat solution of this sort is fairly rare in Lenz.

Five stories may be singled out within this general theme of human relations. 'Nur auf Sardinien' (Only in Sardina, 1953 JdS.) is one of Lenz's very rare excursions into a setting other than Germany or the North. Vittorio is on the run from prison, to which he has been sent unjustly by Don Poddu. Poddu is murdered and, although innocent, Vittorio is accused and the guards are doubled to hunt him. He marries Maddalena before he is caught, but she gives him away, claims the reward for his capture and uses half of it to get the services of a lawyer who, despite Vittorio's lack of co-operation, secures his release. But the young marriage has failed, through the unwillingness of Vittorio to accept that, for however good a reason, his wife had betrayed him. Maddalena fails too to realise what Vittorio's problem is.The twists in the relationship demonstrate Lenz's skill as a story-teller, in a story where there is much tension on the level of pure narrative.

'Silvesterunfall' (Accident on New Year's Eve, 1958 Fs.) and 'Der 6. Geburtstag' (The Sixth Birthday, 1964 Sv.) show us 'macabre festivals', as Colin Russ has appropriately called them.[42] Both 'celebrations' are ironic. The birthday is of a child dying of leukaemia, and the date has been brought forward because it is thought he will not survive until the actual date. The mother fights against drink, buys toys for the sick child, but the game is given away by a piqued elder sister. The child takes no notice, but this is too much for the mother, who breaks the promise not to drink. The ending twists the relationship between husband and wife: the husband breaks away from the wife at the end not because the game has been given away (which he does not know) but because of her drinking. In a situation where *mutual* understanding is vital, it is shown to be impossible. In 'Silvesterunfall', Rudolf, an old waiter, is sixty-four and dying, but is determined to live until his sixty-fifth birthday so that his insurance policies will be paid out in full. At a forced New Year celebration the family play at 'Bleigiessen' (melting scraps of lead and divining from the resultant shapes what the future will hold). The children do this with vague results, but when it is the father's turn, the son, fearing that the outcome might not be so vague, knocks the hot lead out of his hand, burning his own hand badly. The new beginning, that of a new year, is going to be an end. The story is from the *Feuerschiff* collection, as is 'Der Anfang von Etwas', which also takes place at New Year, but which is concerned, not with a real death, but with a supposed one.

'Die Nacht im Hotel' (Night in a Hotel, 1949 JdS.) and 'Ihre Schwester' (Her Sister, 1958 Sv.) also explore human relationships. In the former, perhaps Lenz's earliest story, a man has taken a room at a hotel so that he can travel back by train (as he tells a room-mate he never sees) expressly to wave to his small son as the train passes. The man oversleeps, and returns home in a spirit of failure only to hear that the room-mate, who criticised his deceit, *has* waved to his son. The story is a slight one. 'Ihre Schwester' (originally a dramatised piece for radio, and reminiscent of Faulkner) concerns a young man who, having failed examinations that would have qualified him as a teacher, decides to approach a marriage agency in search of a wife. He meets a girl who

123

claims to be acting on behalf of her sister. The student pretends that he, too, is speaking for someone else, and the story looks as if the two are destined for each other. It is lifted from the purely sentimental not only by the style but also through the customary twist at the end. It emerges that the girl indeed had a sister (Lenz builds up narrative tension by authenticating her existence) but she has been dead for some years, drowned whilst trying to save a pupil during a school outing (the one she is supposed to be on at the moment). The focus shifts then to the girl, who is herself injured, and her obsession with the dead sister. The student decides to try his exams again—the questions that real life puts are too difficult for him.

The theme of failure, seen very clearly in the early novels, is apparent in many of the short stories. Indeed 'Der Läufer' (The Runner, 1951 JdS.) is a kind of sketch for a subsequent novel. The central figure, Fred, puts his last efforts into winning a 5,000 metre race in which he has no chance. But during the course of the race he accidentally spikes one of the other competitors and is disqualified. The failure is again inevitable, and the dominant motif is of the retreat—the starting point of Fred's 'running'. A similar attempt at a comeback is seen in 'Die Mannschaft' (The Team, 1969 Ein.) in which a basketball game is seen alternatively from the viewpoint of the members of the team, and then from Klaus Körner, a star returning after injury. He is fouled and takes his revenge, only to be sent off. This has happened at an equal point, but now the game is lost. Körner does not even stay to see the result. Both 'Der Läufer' and 'Die Mannschaft' echo stories like Hemingway's 'The Undefeated', and the influence of *To Have and Have Not* and *The Old Man and the Sea* have not gone unnoticed. The last words of Harry Morgan in the former are incoherent but comprehensible:

'A man,' Harry Morgan said, looking at them both. 'One man alone ain't got. No man alone now.' He stopped. No matter how a man alone ain't got no bloody chance.'[43]

This alone-ness is seen in several of Lenz's characters, especially in 'Jäger des Spotts' (Hunter of Mockery, JdS.) The date of this is problematic; Lenz's date of 1950 must refer to the original idea of a story in an Eskimo setting, since it has been made clear that the work is very close indeed to *The Old Man and the Sea*.[44] Atoq, after a long period of failure, kills a musk-ox of massive proportions, but is unable to bring it back because it is eaten by bears, and so returns home with the horns. Whether Atoq is ultimately a failure or not is debatable, and he returns not to mockery but to deliberate silence. The main difference from the Hemingway story is that Atoq is still a young man.

'Das Wrack' (The Wreck, 1952), like much of the *Jäger des Spotts* volume, is also influenced by Hemingway. This story echoes Hemingway's 'After the Storm', and if the reasons for the failure to find something on a wreck are different, the theme is similar. Baraby hopes to find his fortune on a wreck he has discovered, but it contains only dead horses. Going beyond Hemingway, 'Das Wrack' permits a reading other than just that of a man tested and failing. The implicit conflict between the father and the son—the latter wanting to forget about the wreck (the past, the war?), and the former insisting—is of some importance. Atoq, too, was impelled by his father's memory.

This sort of conflict is there too in 'Drüben auf den Inseln' (Over on the Islands, 1954 JdS). A young man, not accepted by the island community of the girl with whom he is in love, 'proves himself' by taking out a boat during a storm. He dies, and only at his death is he (silently) accepted. Other failures are of smaller moment. 'Der Beweis' (Proof, 1964 Sv.) shows us a bargee who has been cheated for years on his freight-holdings, and forces people to make an accurate measurement of his barge and its height by crashing it on its last trip. Similar is the foredoomed defence against military power of a landclaim in 'Die Festung' (The Fortress, 1954 JdS,), and the failed comeback of a drunken singer, Barbara Pirchow, who has tried to make this comeback at a ball, but has succeeded only in making a spectacle of herself ('Ball der Wohltäter').

Two final stories in this category may be singled out: 'Stimmungen der See' (Moods of the Sea, 1957 Fs.) and 'Lukas, sanftmütiger Knecht' (Luke the Gentle Servant, 1953 JdS.). In the first, a group of people try to escape from Eastern Europe, after or during the war, and fight against the sea on a supposed route to Sweden. They arrive back after a storm in their own country, to be taken or killed. 'Lukas' has received more attention. Here the scene is Kenya during the Mau-Mau terror, and the basic notion is that the Kikuyus have been driven off land in the past which has been resettled by English farmers. The Kikuyu have returned, servants on their own farm, one of whom is Lukas, the gentle servant, who, with a group of others, takes the English narrator prisoner. He is forced to watch a Mau-Mau ceremony of initiation, and the horror that Lenz sets in motion in the opening paragraph builds up into an image of the burning land. The man is told that he has a certain time to get back to save the farm—Lukas' originally, now his. He struggles against fears and hardships to get back, but:

> The farm was standing no longer, and it was still a good while to sundown. I went to the breadfruit tree and looked at the ashes. I knelt and put my hand into them. The ashes were cold. (JdS., p. 25)

The theme of failure is that of *Es waren Habichte in der Luft*, and we recall again the Ambrose Bierce story of the man who has been hanged, but has the illusion of freedom before the rope jerks tight. The narrator does not know that he has been condemned. There is an historical justice involved here: Lukas has played the rôle of the servant in Brecht's story 'Massnahmen gegen die Gewalt' (Measures against Force, in Brecht's *Keunergeschichten*), the tale of a man who serves a tyrant, but never actually agrees to do so. When the man dies, the servant answers 'no'. On a broader level, the story ranks with the early studies of fated failure, one of Lenz's most strikingly recurrent themes.

8

STAGE AND RADIO PLAYS

Lenz's first play to be staged, *Zeit der Schuldlosen* (Time of the Innocents), which was premièred in the *Deutsches Schauspielhaus* in Hamburg in September 1961, brought him immediate recognition as a dramatist. The play is a combination of two earlier radio plays, *Zeit der Schuldlosen* and *Zeit der Schuldigen* (Time of the Guilty) which were first broadcast in February 1960 and April 1961 respectively. These two plays form the two acts of the later play, which was performed with only minimal changes to the originals.

The play has been subsequently performed in many countries, though an English translation has not been published, and has been acclaimed as 'the most brilliant and the most brutal treatment of the question of guilt which the post-war German theatre has produced.'[45]

But Lenz's qualities as a stage dramatist were not confirmed by his subsequent plays; *Das Gesicht* (The Face, 1964) and *Die Augenbinde* (The Blindfold, 1970) were both received coolly by audiences and critics alike. Lenz has, however, continued to write successful radio plays, though only four are available in printed form in the collection *Haussuchung* (House to House Search).

All of Lenz's stage dramas treat the same theme, and are set against the same political background of a totalitarian régime with which an individual or group of individuals come into conflict. The plays are parables presenting an extreme situation as a testing ground for human morality. As the individuals undergo this test their true characters emerge; the veneer of humanity and sophistication of civilised beings is stripped away to reveal man as an egoistic opportunist, whose labile moral character is manipulated by a world beyond his control. The individual capitulates to force and forfeits his illusion of freedom and self-determination. This dramatic world is one of powerful determining forces in which all belief in man's moral capacity is eroded and destroyed by pressure applied from without, and in which self-preservation replaces heroism. Yet within this world Lenz looks to man to resist, retain his integrity, but in some non-ideological manner. One must act according to conscience, but when one acts out of conviction one approaches fanaticism; the borderline between the two remains problematically obscure and ambiguous, hence the potential dramatic quality of the theme. In this world of continuing relativism, guilt and innocence are reversed with bewildering rapidity.

It is *Zeit der Schuldlosen* which most effectively investigates these issues. When Lenz first started work on this theme it was in the form of a novella which was to deal with the 'adventure of nine men who remained innocent at a time of extreme lawlessness', and to demonstrate how this 'shining innocence, which had been bought by silent approval and looking away, was put to the test and refuted'.[46] The novella was to investigate the nature of innocence, showing how far it was merely a matter of chance. The play extends the theme and introduces the idea of pressure being brought to bear on this innocence and the 'crisis of decision' faced by the nine men when made to choose between the 'alternative of dying, in order to remain innocent, or living and becoming guilty'.

Though the material was developed in dramatic form, the play still bears the stamp of a novella, in that it is based upon and develops out of an initial 'unerhörte Begebenheit' (a remarkable or novel incident, from which the genre takes its name). The incident in this case is the arrest and incarceration of nine completely innocent men, a reversal of the normal order of the world.

These nine men, 'a cross-section of the community', (ZdS., p. 5), are held together with a youth, Sason, who has been arrested after an assassination attempt on the governor of the unidentified state in which they live. The nine men are not named, but referred to simply as a banker, engineer, doctor, student, lorry driver, hotelier, printer, peasant and consul (the latter figure is a Baron in the earlier version). True individuality is not Lenz's concern, nor are the differences between these representative members of society, but rather the strategies with which they approach the problem facing them and, ultimately, when the contingent aspects of personality are pared away, their collective mentality and action.

The nine are assured from the start that no doubt exists in their captors' minds as to their innocence, and it is 'precisely for this reason that they have been chosen'. (ZdS., p. 7) They are to be held captive until they either persuade Sason, who has been interrogated and tortured without success, to reveal the identity of his accomplices, or to abandon his revolutionary cause and agree to work for the governor. Should they fail in this, any third course of action remains open to them to agree upon. They are to be kept there until some satisfactory solution is found; satisfactory, that is, to the state authorities.

It is obvious from the outset that the concept of innocence attached to these nine men is based upon a paradox that stems from the incommensurability of legal and moral innocence, which do not coincide in the world of the play as they would in an ideal world. Their legal innocence, it is implied, constitutes moral guilt. Whilst they are free from any crime committed in or against the state, they are morally guilty of silent complicity in the injustices perpetrated by this dictatorial régime. It is for this reason that they have been chosen. Their crime is that of indifference, non-contention and non-involvement. But now, faced with an extreme situation, and the choice of either demonstrating innocence in an active manner, by resisting the state's use of them as instruments of its will, or incurring guilt by capitulating to the force of the state, their true moral colour is revealed. It is only because they have never before been faced with such a

decision that they have hitherto retained the illusion of innocence; and in this manner the 'chance' nature of their innocence is revealed.

Throughout the first act the characters debate their
dilemma, until an unspoken consensus emerges among them
as to what must be done. Their initial reactions vary: the
printer mutilates himself with a guillotine, cutting off some of
his fingers, hoping thereby to effect his release, but without
success; the peasant simply begs for Sason's sympathy; the
student, who reveals some agreement with Sason's cause,
offers him a poison capsule, in order to release him from
further suffering; the lorry driver employs brute force; the
doctor argues on the grounds of his social importance, dedi-
cated as he is to the same basic cause as Sason, the relief of
suffering; the engineer maintains that they represent the
democratic majority and Sason must bend to their wishes;
the banker argues that Sason has nothing to lose by helping
them; the hotelier suggests a feigned agreement on Sason's
part until they have been released. But Sason is impervious
to all these arguments. He legitimises his action by referring
to the paradox of guilt: 'Today one can only be innocent by
taking a certain guilt upon oneself.' (ZdS., p. 30) He refuses
to betray his cause for the sake of these men. Only by dying
can he remain consistent with his claim to be acting to
achieve greater dignity for mankind. There is a certain logic
in his argument: he maintains that he is fighting on behalf of
human freedom, yet he takes upon himself the right to abuse
the most basic freedom, by choosing to kill. Thus, only his
death will genuinely legitimise his action and prove his dedi-
cation to the cause of freedom:

> If I live our attempt has failed . . . One can choose the wrong
> death—I have chosen this death because it is the only one that I
> can accept. And I beg you to understand me. Naturally I know
> that we would all be free—if I betrayed my friends and my
> conviction. Naturally it is conceivable that I could work for the
> governor. But then I would lose that death that takes away the
> meaninglessness and revulsion from my life. (ZdS., pp. 21–22)

130

Sason is intransigent, firm in his conviction that 'he who wants the best for man must kill or be killed.' (ZdS., p. 30) He not only knows that he will die but wishes to die—and at the hands, directly or indirectly, of the state which he sought to overthrow.

But Sason's stance must not be regarded as simply reflecting an unreserved acceptance on Lenz's part of the need for violent resistance or terrorism. The most persuasive voice in the play is not that of Sason, but of the cynical consul, who continually questions and undermines Sason's idealism. Sason's claim that he is fighting for man's dignity and freedom is dismissed as the banner-cry of many who have used and abused it in the past. Sason's insistence that he will become the proto-martyr of his revolutionary cause is mocked by the consul:

> He's not only an assassin—he wants to be a martyr as well. And they are the most dangerous. . . . All martyrs are, in a certain sense, assassins; they want to preach and convince us that there is something that one must die for. They even demand by their example, that one must be killed. They are in complete agreement with a bloodbath—with the one proviso that this bloodbath must serve sublime and not profane ends. (ZdS., p. 22)

The consul remains cynically detached from the arguments and counter-arguments between the intransigent Sason and the equally intransigent other eight men. He sees the arguments of both sides and the faults of each. He is impervious to Sason's convictions and his rhetoric:

> Strange, he who rests so warmly in the womb of his conviction clearly does not know the horror of doubt; he is complete, he has a ready opinion for everything. Almost admirable—but only almost. (ZdS., p. 39)

Lenz sees doubt as a form of commitment in itself, and this he expresses through this figure who recognises that Sason indeed is here imposing his view upon the group.

The play should not be seen too simply as a parallel to Nazi Germany—this would make decisions and 'sides' too clear-cut, and vindicate views historically. This anonymous state contains injustices but the debate is also upon the problem of whether violent resistance is permissible. Such questions are raised but never answered.

The outcome of this first act is that, during the night, although four of them (the student, the consul, the peasant and doctor) have agreed to keep guard on Sason to prevent his being attacked by the others, Sason is murdered—by whom is not revealed. They are now all free to go, since they have fulfilled the duty the state had expected of them. Unlike Sason, they have not killed out of conviction, but simply out of the desire to be free themselves.

The second act reverses the situation. Sason's revolutionary group have taken power and are carrying out a purge of previous enemies. The eight men (the printer having committed suicide) are re-arrested—not now as innocents, but as guilty men. They stand collectively accused of the murder of Sason. Their action, previously sanctioned by the state as justifiable homicide, now becomes a crime in the eyes of the new state. They become their own judges; and are faced with the ultimatum that they either discover the murderer or be jointly punished. At first they claim to be unable to remember the details, but then they each begin to produce circumstantial evidence that will implicate others and demonstrate their own innocence. Each, it is shown, had good reason to want Sason's death: either because they had pressing engagements to attend to (some of a criminal nature) or because they sought revenge against Sason, or because they were firm supporters and personal friends of the governor. Their arguments are presented, not with the objective of revealing the truth and ensuring that justice is done, but rather in order to seek to exculpate themselves and protect their own selfish interests.

The consul, who now assumes the rôle of the *advocatus diaboli*, frustrates their efforts to legitimise their action and their claim to have acted in the name of a state which not only condoned but also demanded their response:

That's a speciality of our age: murder under orders. He who kills by order can count on extenuating circumstances. It's an odd sort of mentality that cannot understand the person who murders out of greed or passion, but pardons the murderer under orders. (ZdS., p. 58)

Only the student accepts the concept of collective guilt, reminding them:

I shared the same distress, and presumably the same wish as you. My freedom depended on Sason as well. We were all innocent . . . We all became murderers in our imagination . . . when we recognised that Sason would not give up anything: neither the names of his friends nor his conviction. We committed a spiritual crime, but only one carried it out. As strange as it may sound: certain crimes need to be aided and abetted by a mood. We created that mood. Therefore we are guilty. (ZdS., p. 69)

But whilst the consul recognises this, he still holds a sceptical view of Sason's idealism:

Consul: Our assassin committed a murder from conviction. This is one of the strange achievements of our age: he who kills from conviction or in the name of an idea acts legally, at least the supporters of that idea think so.
Hotelier: But that would mean that murder is allowed under certain circumstances. When do these circumstances count, and before what court? (ZdS., p. 74)

The student, who had joined Sason's cause after being released, represents the now prevailing state ideology:

Student (fanatically): There is murder for justice. We, my friends and I, are convinced that the community and the laws that we envisage are worth the lives of a few people. Whoever subscribes to our cause, whoever is prepared to act like us, must take something upon himself.
Consul: Even guilt?
Student: Even guilt. (ZdS., p. 74)

But the student, representative of a fanaticism that is anathema to Lenz, *also* seems to speak with the author's voice

133

when he refers to man's moral responsibility. Asked how any individual can feel responsible for the actions of others the student replies:

> We are. He who decides to live as a witness and silent accomplice of crimes can only do this on condition he feels responsibility. This or death: these are the only justifications. (ZdS., p. 82)

But the consul, agreeing with the feeling of common guilt, cannot accept that one can act on behalf of the group:

> I can't help it, but he who claims to act in the name of everyone always seems to me too presumptuous or stupid. (ZdS., p. 83)

The student in the second act and Sason in the first both take on this rôle of spokesman for the whole of the community. They act from conscience, but this turns into fanaticism as tyrannical and dictatorial as the force they resisted.

The dilemma posed by the second act cannot be resolved since the identity of the murderer cannot be ascertained. The peasant accepts the responsibility because the murder was committed during his watch, but the consul will not allow this and commits suicide with a gun provided by the student with which they are told, if certain, to shoot the person they consider guilty. Neither the peasant nor the consul acts out of personal guilt, but out of a conviction of collective guilt on all their parts.

The world lacks all moral coherence because people never display a true conscience. Those who profess to have conscience are either fanatical like the student, who forces the world out of one dictatorial state into another, sympathetically naive, like the peasant, or irremediably cynical, like the consul. The consul revolts, metaphysically, against the world he lives in and removes himself from it, seeing this as the only way of retaining true innocence. His death extinguishes his despair and sense of guilt, but does not remove the taint of guilt from the group. As the student reminds them at the end of the play: 'The crime is expiated, but the guilt still remains among us.' (ZdS., p. 89)

134

The play discusses this problem of collective guilt, particularly relevant at the time of the trials of Nazi war criminals, but does not end there. Changing political attitudes stress another aspect of the play—the problem of terrorism. Those who claim to act for the betterment of society and greater freedom for man betray an ideological certainty that is, to Lenz's mind, suspect. It is such unshakeable conviction that leads to the abuse of freedom and the tyranny of man over man.

The play is extremely effective. It is a drama of ideas, in which action is reduced to a minimum. The form, that of a debate, is particularly suited to the radio medium it was conceived for, and leaves the debate for the audience to take up. The dialectic of guilt and innocence never ends, but will continue as man's history progresses.

Lenz's next play, *Das Gesicht*, was a disappointing sequel to *Zeit der Schuldlosen*, and has little to commend it. Lenz claims that it is an extension of his first play in the use of an extreme situation to test human potential. (Ges., p. 91) In fact it is a reversal of the extreme situation of the first play; rather than man being exposed to pressure and limitation, the central character here is offered limitless freedom and power without accountability.

Bruno Deutz, an insignificant barber, who bears a strong resemblance to the president of the state, is used by the president to impersonate him because of the threat of an assassination attempt. Having adopted the rôle with some trepidation, Deutz comes to relish the power of his position and is later reluctant to relinquish it. Deutz, who had previously been a member of an underground resistance movement, uses his position to introduce a visionary programme of political reform, but his idealism creates a state more brutal and repressive than before. Unwittingly he is also being used by the president to remove the latter's revolutionary son. But Deutz's reign is only temporary and he is ousted by the president when his usefulness is over.

There are inconsistencies within the play. Deutz is seen by

135

his wife as having always concealed a moral duplicity within him—yet other incidents in the play contradict this completely. Any sort of psychological motivation is absent. Deutz symbolises dictatorial caprice, but this is rendered harmless when the genuine president, equally dictatorial, regains power.

The play lacks any real point—it is not a useful insight into the nature, structure or abuse of power, nor the individual's relationship to the state. The language, as in other of Lenz's writings, tends towards the aphoristic, but here it is platitudes that emerge. The play *is* termed a comedy but the humour, whether of farce, or manners, or verbal jokes, is rather weak.

Lenz returned to the tested formula of *Zeit der Schuldlosen* in his third drama *Die Augenbinde*. A group of individuals is faced with the abuse of power by an authoritarian régime. They are left in a moral dilemma: they must either forfeit their dignity by capitulating to this power, or resist, and, whilst not being able to escape, retain their dignity in opposition to the power. The difference between submission and resistance seems minimal, and purely spiritual—they cannot counter the force, only a Pyrrhic victory is to be achieved.

The action of the play is brief. An anthropological-archaeological expedition stumbles across an unknown tribe. This tribe has a peculiarity—due to an hereditary disorder they are all blind. Occasionally a member of the tribe regains his sight, but is then forced to wear a blindfold until his sight gives way again. The visiting group are held captive and are to be kept segregated from the community until they accept that they must don blindfolds, remove all differences between themselves and the tribe and become fully integrated. If they refuse they will be kept in isolation. In either case, escape is impossible, as their attempts prove.

Some of the group capitulate out of moral, others out of physical weakness; one member is blinded but still refuses to join the community; one resists steadfastly. They are forced to accept the *status quo* or live a life of isolated dissent. But to this is added a wider perspective: the leaders of this community are in fact not blind at all, yet they insist on this equalising factor among all other members of the community. They abuse their power and hold others in subjection by deceit. Manipulation of the blind by the powerful is the theme. There is no escape; no physical resistance is possible, only dissent. The play ends on a partially optimistic note. One of the community who had been forced to wear a blindfold after regaining his sight is encouraged by the resistance of two figures from the expedition and rebels, by tearing off his blindfold. Although it is too late, he is already blind, the first hint of a change of attitude, of a revolt against 'blind' subjection to what appears to be an equal yet deceptive force, has emerged.

Blindness, it is suggested, is a means of relieving oneself of moral responsibility; the blindness is a defect common to all communities. It reduces everyone to the same level, individuality and individual responsibility are hidden beneath collective action.

The play was not successful when produced. Though it has the same dramatic quality of concentrated debate as the first play, the theme did not appeal. In the decade between *Zeit der Schuldlosen* and *Die Augenbinde*, German society had grown to believe in its own maturity and did not feel it required reminding of its need to resist manipulation. The events of 1968 had demonstrated dissent to a sufficient degree. What audiences and critics were looking for was some pointer forward and not allegories of the German past.

Lenz's radio plays are on the whole not as abstractly political and philosophical as his stage dramas. Within the radio medium Lenz develops a skill that is close to that of his stories; his plays have a narrative quality and the action lacking in his stage dramas.

The first of these, *Das schönste Fest der Welt* (The Greatest Celebration in the World, 1954), is a satire on social privilege. Set in Portugal, the Marquis da Serpa organises an extravagant party to which the world's leading socialites are invited. The Marquis, more evocative of the *ennui* of a Schnitzler character from the *fin de siècle* than the modern jet-set he associates with, spins a web of opulence above the abyss of his own futility. He surrounds himself with artificiality—the castle park is decorated with concrete swans and frogs. His guests are similarly afflicted—they are snobs or aspiring starlets, confidence tricksters, thieves, all pursuing some elusive and illusory happiness. But beyond the bounds of the castle garden, there exists a village of ordinary, poor peasants, two of whom, angered at this offensive display of wealth and extravagance, infiltrate the castle garden and threaten to blow it up. The Marquis accepts this challenge, which brings a little stimulation and precarious exhilaration into his otherwise stale existence. He is convinced that when they taste of the many pleasures on offer at the celebration their revolutionary zeal will fade. One of them resists the temptations, but his plan fails when the butler removes the main fuses. However, the Marquis adopts the rôle of saboteur and detonates the charges himself. Oppelsheimer, the cynic, sums up the mood of a decadent world bent on self-destruction:

> All of us here are celebrating our own decline. All of us are enjoying ourselves at the cost of a catastrophe. Except for two . . . they belong to those who will celebrate after us. Our evening will be their morning. What I see here my friend has the peculiarity of being a wake and a birthday party at the same time. (Haus., p. 24)

The play also turns around the theme of identity and self-delusion. The two revolutionaries win first prizes at the masked ball, their dishevelled, semi-nude appearance being mistaken as some form of primitive costume joke. Oppelsheimer again delivers a bleak prognosis:

> Your guests think it's a joke. If I'm not mistaken, one day our world will come to an end like this. The warning that comes from above will not be heard for the laughter and applause. We'll greet the catastrophe like a joke. (Haus., p. 31)

138

A violent tirade by one of the revolutionaries is accepted as part of a cabaret display:

> Yes, laugh. Just look at yourselves: you walk around as if you were stuffed. You wear masks so that you won't be bored by each other's faces. (Laughter) Because you can't stand to be alone, you always have to be on the move, enjoying yourselves. Two hours alone and you're ready for the nut-house. (Cries of delight) . . . Shall I tell you what you need? Proper amusement! And do you know what that is? Work, that's what it is, sixty hours in the lead mines over in Tuntasola . . . (Laughter, applause) Stop laughing! You can't even tell them the truth . . . they just laugh. (Haus., p. 36)

Thematically the play can be linked with Max Frisch's *Biedermann und die Brandstifter* (The Fire-Raisers): there is the same warning and danger of blindness, the same provocation, and finally the same self-destruction, though here it results from boredom, rather than stupidity.

The two classes are compared: the healthy, natural peasant, his life geared to the mundane needs of life, and the decadent rich (or opportunists) whose lives appear futile, senseless, pursuing pleasure and activity to escape their own vacuity. The play was an apposite comment in the years of growing affluence and the economic miracle. It is not a drama of revolution but a warning against the pernicious effect of materialism which creates artificial lives and destroys natural authenticity.

The theme of identity is also found in *Haussuchung* (House-to-House Search, 1963). The search is made of a flat where, it is believed, a student has hidden large doses of drugs that have been stolen from local chemists. The search is unsuccessful, but reveals other aspects of the household not obvious to the outside world. Christina has taken the student as her lover. He has stolen the drugs in order to put them in the town's drinking water, to sedate the inhabitants so that he may be alone with Christina. The student is an example of romantic egoism which wishes to deny the reality of everything other than the self and its libidinous desires. Christina's husband is fêted by the town as a hero for acts of bravery at the end of the war. But, it is revealed, this was a case of mistaken identity. He accepts the praise whilst paying small sums to the genuine hero to buy his silence. The husband deceives the world, the wife deceives the husband, and the student wishes to deceive himself that only he and his mistress exist.

Die Enttäuschung (The Disappointment, 1966) shows Lenz's strength as a writer of comedy, here under the influence of Dylan Thomas. This play, set in a prison, uses two voices as narrators.

They describe the waking prison:

> *Second voice:* On the iron, step-worn platform, nervous as a trout, is Herr Barmeister, the youngest warder in Isenbüttel . . . He likes peas and the sound of the harmonium. In passing he strokes the heavy, heavenly, comfortingly cold bolts . . . Herr Barmeister is also the youngest member of the Hamburg Society for the Prevention of Cruelty to Animals and in his spare time prevents acts of violence against Siamese cats, chickens, gold fish, lizards and St. Bernards . . . Now he's inspecting the sleeping Herr Buntje who declared all the thatched cottages of Schleswig his personal enemies and used as his only weapon the match . . . Next to him, silently whistling, Lord Stickyfingers is combing his hair in a broken piece of mirror. His Lordship had been an accountant and could not understand why the money from the Büggelin company was so attached to him that it stuck. (Haus., p. 41)

It is the morning of a big occasion. A visiting theatre company is to perform a play, 'The Disappointment', and some of the captive audience are to take the parts of extras. The world of the play and reality merge. The play within a play deals with two wreckers who lure boats on to the rocks in the hope of rich pickings. But the cargo proves to be nothing more than a number of wild animals, played by the prisoners. They intend to use the play as a cover for an escape attempt. Unfortunately their rôles in the play predict that they be forced back into the ship's hold and, despite attempts to resist the force employed against them, the reality of the play prevails.

140

Lenz shows great skill in the invention of comic characters and an exuberant delight in the musicality of language. The play is a humorous look at some of life's failures and a comic variation on the theme of the prison of life and its literally inescapable determining rôle.

The black comedy *Das Labyrinth* (The Labyrinth, 1967) is also a humorous treatment of one of Lenz's serious themes, that of dictatorial attitudes, seen here in a grotesquely distorted form of women's liberation that is reminiscent of *Arsenic and Old Lace*.

Two sisters, confessed misogamists, have in their possession a labyrinth which has the remarkable power of making anyone who enters it disappear. At the suggestion of an aunt they decide to put this capacity to use in their campaign against oppressive husbands. Believing it to be a man's world they decide to solve the problem not by correcting the imbalance but by eradicating the opposition. They face intolerance with an equal but opposite intolerance.

Their task they see as woman's redemption, and declare a Holy War against men. Their fanaticism has the dimensions of political extremism, and their speeches the rhetoric of self-styled saviours:

> With the help of the labyrinth we will achieve salvation, many small salvations . . . We have been given a sign, we must recognise it . . . the time of humble suffering will end . . . The time of insults and silent submission . . . The time of secret tears . . . It is in our hands to make Hamburg, or part of Hamburg happy again. (Haus., p. 81)

They despatch a number of husbands but later it is revealed that their androphobia is really due to disappointment in love, and is a form of compensatory revenge. When the sisters' former lover returns the more militant sister flees with him into the labyrinth to escape the world and the other's rivalry.

The abstract debate of the stage dramas is replaced in the radio plays by a stronger concentration on character and

141

action. But the characters are absurd rather than real and throw light, through their distortion, on aspects of modern life, particularly that of self-delusion. Characters attempt to determine reality or their own rôles in life, but what emerge are deceit, obsession and egoistic passions. Lenz is one of the most-performed radio dramatists with this blending of the entertaining and the problematic. His tendency to moralise is balanced by his humorous sympathy with life's failures.

9

CONCLUSION

It is difficult to make concluding remarks about an author in mid-career. Indeed the very finality of a conclusive judgement would be one that is, significantly, anathema to Lenz himself, since he considers himself a witness to the world, and the German past, but never its judge. Just as his literary characters experience life as an unstable reality, so too the reality of Lenz's work will continue to be re-interpreted in the light of social and political developments.

Lenz insists that a story may be told in many ways, each having an element of truth in it. For this reason he adopts the attitude of the uncommitted, sceptical observer of the tragedy of life, attempting to retain a difficult neutrality where others would express personal judgements. Existence for Lenz is a matter of decisions, of borderline situations, of moves from passive to active being, in a world that is presented as physically hostile and its people morally labile. If man takes up the challenge of life he either reveals a momentary dignity, or heroism, in attempting to face irrational forces with strength or determination (as in the early novels and stories) or he attempts to make a moral stand, and runs the risk of becoming the very tyrannical force he is resisting.

Guilt is the strongest feature of life, and this albeit non-theological guilt is based upon a belief in humanity as an end in itself. There is no transcendent element in Lenz's world, other than that of history. His concern is human freedom. However, as soon as this basic belief expresses itself in some form of action, Lenz considers, it endangers itself by becoming its own antithesis—the restriction of human freedom, the tyrannical imposition of a fixed judgement and the

143

endeavour to force this view upon others. For Lenz, fanaticism begins where innocence ends, but innocence can also be suspect: a state of being where the challenge of life has not yet been felt.

Lenz, as an uncompromising moralist, places upon everyone the responsibility for the state of the world, where theological doctrines and political ideologies might relieve one of such responsibility. In common with many of his contemporaries, he is aware of the dangers of the seductive certainty of firm political belief. Relativism is the key to Lenz's world; today's saviours are tomorrow's despots. Within this ever-changing reality Lenz identifies with only one philosophical certainty, that of doubt: when one doubts the nature of reality, one affirms that same reality in all its contradictory manifestations. Lenz in his explicit and implicit questioning of truth comes near to stating that there *is* no truth—but this provides its own contradiction in any affirmation of its own veracity. This is the only paradoxical certainty in Lenz's view of the world.

When Lenz moved away from his literary model, Hemingway, he explained that he had previously presented in his writings only physical, momentary confrontations, as documents of human failure. Later he recognised in the world the presence of a 'verändernde Intelligenz' (an intelligence that causes change, Bez., p. 44). This reference, not to a higher destiny or divine grace, appears to be a development away from the sometime cruel, at all times inescapable determinism of his early work. But this is not really the case. In the later works the physical struggle is augmented by the moral dilemma. The determining forces in the moral sphere are a parallel to those of physical existence. The change that Lenz refers to is not a true progression, and certainly not progress, but a cyclical movement, as figures vie for the rôle of dominant force.

In order to escape the demands of life, the dangers of commitment (to however noble a cause), people like Siggi Jepsen attempt to find a refuge from the world, but this is only the apparent innocence of the figures in *Zeit der Schuldlosen*. Non-involvement is impossible within Lenz's rigorous morality.

Lenz protests against the inhumanity of his fellow beings, but he is not programmatic in suggesting a re-ordering of the world that might diminish such faults. His writings are not the violent protest of the political activist, but the resigned gesture of a generation that has witnessed an obsession with mass ideology and visionary political programmes. Lenz defends the politics of dissent, indirectly at least, but remains aware of the dangers that such a negative creed implies. Sceptical, ironical, occasionally satirical, he fears the trap of self-righteousness.

His success lies in being able to activate the reader's conscience, and the German conscience, without claiming his own moral superiority. He is a guardian against complacency, and (still) a witness to the past. Moderation may be applicable (were the term not all too relative in the modern age) to the dominating tone of his work and the animating personality behind it. He is an uneasy presence in a society which might wish to shrug off the lessons of the past in the belief that they inhabit a better world where such excesses are inconceivable.

It must be recalled, too, that Lenz is not entirely preoccupied in his writings with themes of guilt. The opposite theme, that of innocence, is there too, and is most clearly apparent in the Suleyken stories, which portray a world in which the people never reflect (and as far as guilt is concerned, nor does Lehmann, for all his criminal activities). Lenz is aware that the world of Suleyken is lost, and that Bollerup is threatened, but the fact that he can tell just this sort of story with an accurate and entertaining touch is something of importance, and Lenz will be remembered, perhaps, as the creator of Suleyken as well as of Rugbüll.

It is, of course, impossible in a short study to convey more than an impression of a writer's style or skill. But it is nevertheless appropriate to conclude with Lenz as a story-

145

teller, since this is perhaps what he does best of all, and what continues to make him a best-seller. Lenz has a sure eye, and not only in the humorous stories, for what will entertain: passages might be pointed to in *Deutschstunde* and *Das Vorbild* where the same entertainment comes through. A writer's ability to tell a story, to entertain, to create tension and hold the attention of the reader is sometimes neglected, or even frowned upon by the literary critics. Yet precisely these features—and Lenz *is* a good storyteller—are surely the preliminary requirement for any literature.

NOTES

1 *Siegfried Lenz—Baumeister einer brüderlichen Welt,* Bauhütten, Hamburg, 1970, pp. 30–40.
2 Figures from *Deutsche Bestseller—Deutsche Idologie,* ed. H. L. Arnold, Klett, Stuttgart, 1975, p. 90.
3 See the bibliography for the various versions of these essays.
4 S. Lenz, *Flug über Land und Meer,* Westermann, Brunswick, 1967, p. 7.
5 Thus G. P. Butler in *The Times Literary Supplement,* 29 April 1977, p. 536.
6 Many of the articles in the *Text und Kritik* volume devoted to Lenz (see bibliography) take this tone, but see M. Gregor-Dellin's response in *Die Zeit,* 3 December 1976, p. 17.
7 *Der Friede und die Unruhestifter,* ed. H. J. Schulz, Suhrkamp, Frankfurt/M., 1973, pp. 335–44, esp. p. 340 f.
8 M. Reich-Ranicki, 'Siegfried Lenz—der gelassene Mitwisser,' first in *Deutsche Literatur in West und Ost,* Piper, Munich, 1963, pp. 69–84, then in C. Russ, *Der Schriftsteller Siegfried Lenz,* Hoffmann und Campe, Hamburg, 1973, pp. 215–28.
9 'Gediegene Deutschstunde für die ganze Welt', *Der Spiegel,* XXX (1976) Nr. 12 (15.3.76), p. 97.
10 A. Bierce, *In the Midst of Life,* Penguin, Harmondsworth, 1939, pp. 29–31. The work has been filmed several times.
11 'Vom Terror gehetzt,' *Frankfurter Allgemeine Zeitung,* 21 April 1951 (also in G. Uhlig, *Autor, Werk und Kritik III,* Hueber, Munich, 1972, p. 99 f.).
12 H. Wagener, *Siegfried Lenz,* Beck, Munich, 1976, p. 22.
13 W. J. Schwarz, *Der Erzähler Siegfried Lenz,* Francke, Berne and Munich, 1974, pp. 23–5.
14 'The Cherries of Freedom', first published in 1952 by the Frankfurter Verlagsanstalt, Frankfurt/M.
15 Wagener, *Lenz,* p. 30 recalls Heinrich Böll's *Und sagte kein einziges Wort* here, and Lenz has indeed singled that novel out himself.

16 See R. Gessmann, 'Sport als Motiv in der Literatur,' *Literatur in Wissenschaft und Unterricht,* VI (1973), 143–55, esp. p. 144, and E. Mornin, 'Taking Games Seriously,' *Germanic Review,* LI (1976), 278–95.

17 'Entstehungsgeschichte eines Sportromans,' (The Genesis of a Sport-Novel, 1960), quoted here from *Dichter deuten den Sport I,* ed. K. Schwarz, Hofmann, Schondorf bei Stuttgart, 1967, p. 97 f. Schwarz lists other writings by Lenz on sport, as does Mornin, 'Games,' p. 278, n.1. There are essays on sport in Bez., pp. 176–87.

18 Wagener, *Lenz,* p. 37.

19 The symbolism is well discussed in an article echoed frequently by later criticism: H. Lehnert, 'Die Form des Experiments als Gleichnis,' *Frankfurter Hefte,* XVIII (1963), 476.

20 Lehnert, 'Form,' p. 477.

21 There is a certain artificiality here and the section has come in for criticism on the grounds that these are cardboard figures uttering platitudes: thus Wagener, *Lenz,* p. 50.

22 Lehnert, 'Form,' pp. 478–81.

23 Wagener, *Lenz,* p. 78 and others have drawn attention to the proximity to the novella form.

24 This is the main thesis of Elm's study, *Siegfried Lenz: 'Deutschstunde,'* Fink, Munich, 1974.

25 See E. Loewy, *Literatur unterm Hakenkreuz,* Fischer, Frankfurt am Main and Hamburg, 1969, p. 130.

26 Wagener, *Lenz,* p. 99.

27 It is enlightening to look at Ludwig Tieck's introduction to the *Denkwürdige Geschichtschronik der Schildbürger* of 1796, in *Ludwig Tieck I. Dichter über ihre Dichtungen* 9/I, Heimeran, Munich, 1971, pp. 98–103.

28 Jean Paul, *Quintus Fixlein (Erster Zettelkasten),* in *Jean Pauls Werke,* Aufbau, Berlin, 1968, I, 165 f.

29 Wagener, *Lenz,* p. 101.

30 We might note that other tales by Lenz are set in Masuria but are not humorous (an example is *Lotte soll nicht sterben,* referred to in Chapter 1), and there are other stories about the area near Suleyken; for example the school reader *Das Wunder von Striegeldorf* (The Miracle of Striegeldorf), Hirschgraben, Frankfurt/M., 3. ed., 1973, contains two of these.

31 The link with *Deutschstunde* is noted by J-J. Schuhmacher in

reviewing the Bollerup stories in *Allemagnes d'aujourd'hui*, LVI (January–February 1977), 84–6.

32   Wagener, *Lenz*, p. 104.

33   Killy, 'Gediegene Deutschstunde,' p. 201 f.

34   See K. Kusengerg, 'Über die Kurzgeschichte,' included in *Theorie der Kurzgeschichte*, ed. H. C. von Nayhaus, Reclam, Stuttgart, 1977, pp. 33–40. The collection contains an abridged version of Lenz's essay, which is printed in Bez., and elsewhere.

35   G. Grack, review of *Der Spielverderber* in: *Neue deutsche Hefte*, XIV (1967), I, 124–7.

36   The essay—in Bez, as 'Mein Vorbild Hemingway' (My Model, Hemingway)—originated as a radio feature in a series called 'Modell oder Provokation' (Model or Provocation); see *Fünfzehn Autoren suchen sich selbst*, ed. U. Schulz, List, Munich, 1967, pp. 9–20.

37   See Anthony Burgess' excellent review of A. E. Hotchner's *Papa Hemingway*, New York, 1966, 'He Wrote Good' in: *Urgent Copy*, Penguin, Harmondsworth, 1973, pp. 34–8.

38   See E. W. Trahan's introduction to her collection *Gruppe 47*, Blaisdell, Waltham/Mass., 1969, pp. ix–xvi, and the more recent book by S. Mandel, *Group 47*, Southern Illinois UP, Carbondale/Edwardsville, 1973.

39   *Erzähler*, p. 45.

40   Compare the DTV collection of Böll's satires, *Nicht nur zur Weihnachtszeit*, Munich, 1966, which contains several stories close to those of Lenz.

41   *Interpretationen zu Siegfried Lenz*, Oldenbourg, Munich, 3. ed., 1973, pp. 67–74.

42   C. Russ, 'The Macabre Festival,' in: *Deutung und Bedeutung*, ed. B. Schludermann et al., Mouton, The Hague, 1973, pp. 275–93.

43   Ernest Hemingway, *To Have and Have Not*, Penguin, Harmondsworth, 1975, p. 178.

44   See S. Kirschner, 'From the Gulf Stream into the Main Stream,' *Research Studies*, XXXV (1967), 141–7.

45   H. Beissel, 'Between Two Nightmares: The German Theatre after World War Two,' *Seminar*, I (1965) 55–68 (p. 64).

46   'Mein erstes Theaterstück. Wie "Zeit der Schuldlosen" enstand,' in: *Zeit der Schuldlosen—Zeit der Schuldigen*, ed. A. R. Schmitt, Appleton-Century-Crofts, New York, 1967, pp. 7–10.

149

SELECT BIBLIOGRAPHY

Writings by and on Lenz are numerous, although less so than it appears at first, since primary and secondary texts have often appeared in several forms. Even so, this bibliography is necessarily selective. The primary works noted are the main ones, with a few others that have been discussed in the text. Tapes and films of the works are not noted, nor are book-club or special editions, school texts, or anthologies with contributions by Lenz. Most of the uncollected stories and essays are excluded, as are most of the afterwords by Lenz to other literature, and all but a few of his interviews. Stories and essays which may be found in the collected volumes are not usually listed in their original form, broadcast or published. Secondary literature concentrates on the most important and most readily accessible texts, with a few others used in this study. Articles in collective volumes are not listed separately. For fuller bibliographies, see the studies by Bassmann and Schwarz, the collection edited by Russ, and the *Text und Kritik* volume. All are noted in section II below (general studies). Unless otherwise stated, Lenz's works are published by Hoffmann and Campe in Hamburg. Paperback editions are given in brackets.

I WORKS BY LENZ

Novels

Es waren Habichte in der Luft, 1951 (DTV, Munich, 1965).
Duell mit dem Schatten, 1953.
Der Mann im Strom, 1957 (DTV, Munich, 1963).
Brot und Spiele, 1959 (DTV, Munich, 1964).
Stadtgespräch, 1963 (DTV, Munich, 1965).
Deutschstunde, 1968 (DTV, Munich, 1973).
Das Vorbild, 1973.

Die frühen Romane, (Afterword by K. G. Just), 1976 (=Hab., Mann, Brot, Stg.)

Short stories

So zärtlich war Suleyken, 1955 (Fischer, Frankfurt/M., 1960).
Jäger des Spotts, 1958 (DTV, Munich, 1965).
Das Feuerschiff, 1960 (DTV, Munich, 1966).
Lehmanns Erzählungen, oder So schön war mein Markt. Aus den Bekenntnissen eines Schwarzhändlers, 1964.
Der Spielverderber, 1965 (DTV, Munich, 1969).
Der Geist der Mirabelle. Geschichten aus Bollerup, 1975.
Einstein überquert die Elbe bei Hamburg, 1975.
Gesammelte Erzählungen. (Afterword by C. Russ), 1970.
So war es mit dem Zirkus. Fünf Geschichten aus Suleyken, Mit Bildern von Klaus Warwas, 1971 (DTV, Munich, 1975).
Stimmungen der See, Reclam, Stuttgart, 1962 (=5 stories later included in JdS., Fs., and Sp.).
'*Jäger des Spotts' und andere Erzählungen*, ed. R. H. Spaethling, Norton, New York, 1965 (=5 stories from JdS., and Sul.).
'*Das Wrack' and Other Stories*, ed. C. Russ, Heinemann, London, 1967 (=11 stories from JdS., Fs., and Sp.).
Lotte soll nicht sterben, Grafisk, Copenhagen, 1970 (=adapted form of a story which appeared first in the *Ostpreussenblatt*, 1953, then in a collection called *Begegnungen mit Tieren*, with stories by H. Bender and W. Bergengruen, Hamburger Lesehefte, Hamburg, 1972).
Das Wunder von Striegeldorf, 3. ed., Hirschgraben, Frankfurt/M., 1973 (=3 stories from JdS., with two of the many uncollected Masurian stories).

Essays and portraits

Das Kabinett der Konterbande, 1956 (on the publishers Hoffmann and Campe).
Wippchens charmante Scharmützel, erträumt von Julius Stettenheim, in Erinnerung gebracht von Siegfried Lenz und Egon Schramm, 1960 (Fischer, Frankfurt/M., 1960).
'Entstehungsgeschichte eines Sportromans'(1960), in: *Dichter deuten den Sport*, ed. K. Schwarz, Hofmann, Schorndorf bei Stuttgart, 1967, vol I, pp. 97–98 (on *Brot und Spiele*, originally in *Stadion* LX, 1960, 104 f.).

'Mein erstes Theaterstück. Wie "Zeit der Schuldlosen" entstand,' in: *Die Zeit*, 22.9.61; also in the edition of the play by Schmitt: see below).

Flug über Land und Meer (with Dieter Seelmann), Westermann, Brunswick, 1967.

Leute von Hamburg, 1968.

Beziehungen. Ansichten und Bekenntnisse zur Literatur, 1970 (DTV, Munich, 1972) (=major collection of essays).

Die Herrschaftssprache der CDU, Wählerinitiative Nord, Kiel, 1971.

Verlorenes Land—gewonnene Nachbarschaft. Zur Ostpolitik der Bundesreigierung, Wählerinitiative Nord, Kiel, 1972.

Wo die Möwen schreien (with Dieter Seelmann), Christian, Hamburg, 1976.

Autobiography

'Autobiographische Skizze.' Originally in: Siegfried Lenz, *Stimmungen der See*, Reclam, Stuttgart, 1962, pp. 76–8; revised in: *Siegfried Lenz: Ein Prospekt*, 1966, pp. 11–14; Neis, *Erläuterungen zu den Erzählungen*, 1972, pp. 5–8; Uhlig, *Autor, Werk und Kritik*, 1972, pp. 86–8; Schwarz, *Der Erzähler Siegfried Lenz*, 1974, pp. 5–7. Details of these works in section II.

'Ich zum Beispiel. Kennzeichen eines Jahrgangs' in: *Beziehungen* (see above) and in English translation—see section III.

'Die Schärfe der Kufen,' in: *Atlas, zusammengestellt con deutschen Autoren*, Wagenbach, Berlin, 1965, pp. 9–26.

'Erste Leseerlebnisse,' in: *Erste Leseerlebnisse,* ed. S. Unseld, Suhrkamp, Frankfurt/M., 1975, p. 73–8.

Interviews

'Interview mit Marcel Reich-Ranicki,' (1969), in: *Beziehungen.*

(With Ekkehart Rudolph) in: *Protokoll zur Person*, ed. E. Rudolph, List, Munich, 1971, pp. 95–103.

(With Manès Sperber) in: *Wir und Dostojewskij*, Eine Debatte . . . geführt von M. Sperber, Hoffmann und Campe, Hamburg, 1972, pp. 73–85.

(With Martin Gregor-Dellin) in: *Bücherkommentare XXII*, (1973), Nr. 4, p. 24. Updated in the *Text und Kritik* volume.

'Was kann man schreibend für den Frieden tun? Ein Gespräch zwischen Gustav Heinemann und Siegfried Lenz,' in: *Der*

Friede und die Unruhestifter, ed, H. J. Schulz, Suhrkamp, Frank-furt/M., 1973, pp. 335–44.

(With Alexander Bauer) in: 'Der Autor ist kein Zierfisch,' in: *Bücherkommentare* XXV, (1975), Nr. 1, pp. 1–2.

(With Ekkehart Rudolph) in: *Aussage zur Person*, ed. E. Rudolph, Erdmann, Tübingen, 1977. Pre-print in the *Börsenblatt für den deutschen Buchhandel* LXXI (6.9.77), 7–12.

Radio plays

Das schönste Fest der Welt. (Afterword by C. Ferber), Hans-Bredow-Institut, Hamburg, 1956.

Zeit der Schuldlosen—Zeit der Schuldigen. (Afterword by E. Schramm), Hans-Bredow-Institut, Hamburg, 1961. The radio version is also ed. A. R. Schmitt, with an introduction by Sieg-fried Lenz, Appleton-Century-Crofts, New York, 1967.

Haussuchung. (Afterword by H. Schwitzke), 1967 (DTV, Munich, 1970) (=*Haussuchung, Das schönste Fest der Welt, Die Enttäuschung, Das Labyrinth*).

Das schönste Fest der Welt. Haussuchung, Reclam, Stuttgart, 1970.

Dramas

Zeit der Schuldlosen. (Afterword by J. Bartsch), Kiepenheuer und Witsch, Cologne, 1962. The stage adaptation of the double radio play is also ed. by P. Prager, Harrap, London, 1966. Prager lists a number of unpublished radio plays and features.

Das Gesicht, 1964.

Die Augenbinde. Nicht alle Förster sind froh, Rowohlt, Reinbek bei Hamburg, 1970.

II SECONDARY LITERATURE

General studies

H. Ahl, 'Ein männliches Talent—Siegfried Lenz,' in: *Literarische Portraits*, Langen und Müller, Munich and Vienna, 1962, pp. 36–43.

W. Bassmann, *Siegfried Lenz*, Bouvier, Bonn, 1976.

N. Casanova, 'Siegfried Lenz—Distances et Contacts,' *Allemagnes d'aujourd'hui*, XXXII (March-April, 1972), 32–48.

W. Killy, 'Gediegene Deutschstunde für die ganze Welt,' *Der Spiegel*, XXX (1976) Nr. 12 (15.3.76), 196–202.

H. Lachinger, 'Siegfried Lenz' in: *Deutsche Literatur seit 1945 in Einzeldarstellungen*, ed. D. Weber, Kröner, Stuttgart, 1968, pp. 412–34.

Siegfried Lenz, Text und Kritik, LII (1976) (Essays and a bibliography, See the review by M. Gregor-Dellin in *Die Zeit*, 3.12.76. p. 17, however).

Siegfried Lenz—Baumeister einer brüderlichen Welt. Dokumente einer Ehrung, Bauhütten, Hamburg, 1970 (Speeches about and by Lenz on the occasion of the award of the Literaturpreis der deutschen Freimaurer 1970).

Siegfried Lenz: Ein Prospekt, Hoffmann und Campe, Hamburg, 1966 (Essays, extracts and brief critical appraisals).

H. Pätzold, *Theorie und Praxis moderner Schreibweisen am Beispiel von Siegfried Lenz und Helmut Heissenbüttel*, Bouvier, Bonn, 1977.

M. Reich-Ranicki, 'Siegfried Lenz—der gelassene Mitwisser,' in: *Deutsche Literatur in West und Ost*, Piper, Munich, 1963, pp. 169–84 (and in Russ, *Schriftsteller*, below).

T. Reber, *Siegfried Lenz*, Colloquium, Berlin, 1973 (slight).

C. Russ, 'Siegfried Lenz,' in: *Deutsche Dichter der Gegenwart*, ed. B. von Wiese, Schmidt, Berlin, 1973, pp. 545–59.

C. Russ (ed.), *Der Schriftsteller Siegfried Lenz*, Hoffmann und Campe, Hamburg, 1973 (major collection of essays).

W. J. Schwarz, *Der Erzähler Siegfried Lenz*. (Mit einem Beitrag 'Das szenische Werk' von H.-J. Greif), Francke, Berne and Munich, 1974.

G. Uhlig, *Autor, Werk und Kritik III. Wolfgang Köppen und Siegfried Lenz*, Hueber, Munich, 1972 (extracts from the major works, summaries and brief critical comments).

H. Wagener, *Siegfried Lenz*, Beck, Munich, 1976.

Early novels

K. Batt, 'Geschichten kontra Geschichte. Über die Erzählungen und Romane von Siegfried Lenz,' *Sinn und Form*, XXVI (1974), 847–59.

R. Gessmann, 'Sport als Motiv in der Literatur,' *Literatur in Wissenschaft und Unterricht*, VI (1973), 143–55.

K. G. Just, 'Siegfried Lenz als Erzähler,' *Wirkendes Wort*, XVI (1966), 112–24 (also in *Siegfried Lenz : Ein Prospekt*, above).

H. Lehnert, 'Die Form des Experiments als Gleichnis,' *Frankfurter Hefte*, XVIII (1963), 474–82.

E. Morin, 'Taking Games Seriously. Observations on the German Sport-Novel,' *Germanic Review*, LI (1976), 278–95.

Deutschstunde

W. Beutin, *'Deutschstunde' von Siegfried Lenz. Eine Kritik*, Lüdke, Hamburg, 1970.

J. Drews, 'Siegfried Lenz: *Deutschstunde*,' *Neue Rundschau*, LXXX (1969), 362–6.

T. Elm, *Siegfried Lenz: 'Deutschstunde,' Engagement und Realismus im Gegenwartsroman*, Fink, Munich, 1974.

A. Gisselbrecht, *'Deutschstunde* de Siegfried Lenz: un "classique allemand" de 1968,' *Allemagnes d'aujourd'hui*, XLVI/VII (January–April 1975), 120–7.

P. Härtling, 'Eine Eins für Siggi,' *Der Spiegel*, XXII (1968) Nr. 44 (28.10.68), 178.

E. Neis, *Erläuterungen zu Siegfried Lenz: 'Deutschstunde,'* Bange, Hollfeld/Obfr., 2. ed., 1975.

R. H. Paslick, 'Narrowing the Distance: Siegfried Lenz's *Deutschstunde*,' *German Quarterly*, XLVI (1973), 210–8.

P. Russel, 'Siegfried Lenz's *Deutschstunde*: A North German Novel,' *German Life and Letters*, XXVIII (1974/75), 405–18.

P. Russel, 'The "Lesson" in Siegfried Lenz's *Deutschstunde*,' *Seminar*, XIII (1977), 42–54.

A. Weber, *Siegfried Lenz: 'Deutschstunde.'* (Mit Beiträgen von B. Alt und H. Rickeling), Oldenbourg, Munich, 1971.

W. Weber, 'Siegfried Lenz: *Deutschstunde*,' in: *Forderungen, Bemerkungen und Aufsätze zur Literatur*, Artemis, Zurich and Stuttgart, 1970, pp. 172–8.

H. Worm-Kaschuge, *Lenz. 'Deutschstunde,'* Bange, Hollfeld/Obfr., 2. ed., 1977.

Das Vorbild

W. Ross, 'Vorbilder—leicht beschädigt,' *Merkur*, XXVIII (1974), 188–91.

G. Schramm, 'Wiedererkennen der Wirklichkeit. Über *Das Vorbild* von Siegfried Lenz,' in: *Deutsche Bestseller—Deutsche Ideologie. Ansätze zu einer Verbraucherpoetik*, ed. H. L. Arnold, Klett, Stuttgart, 1975, pp. 90–112.

Short stories

G. Butler, Review of *Einstein überquert die Elbe bei Hamburg*, *Times Literary Supplement* 29.4.77, p. 536.

E. N. Elstun, 'How it seems and how it is: Marriage in Three Stories by Siegfried Lenz,' *Orbis Litterarum*, XXIX (1974), 170–9.

G. Grack, Review of *Der Spielverderber*, *Neue deutsche Hefte*, XIV (1967), Nr. 1, 124–7.

W. P. Hanson, Recorded talk on *Stimmungen der See* and *Der seelische Ratgeber*, Exeter University, Exeter Tapes, 1973.

W. P. Hanson, 'Siegfried Lenz's Short Story *Die Festung*,' *Modern Languages*, XLV (1974), 26–32.

Interpretationen zu Siegfried Lenz, verfasst von einem Arbeitskreis, Oldenbourg, Munich, 3. ed. 1973 (important essays on six stories from JdS., Fs., Sp.).

S. Kirshner, 'From the Gulf Stream into the Main Stream, Siegfried Lenz and Hemingway,' *Research Studies*, XXXV (1967), 141–7.

B. Murdoch, 'Ironic Reversal in the Short Stories of Siegfried Lenz,' *Neophilologus*, LVIII (1974), 406–10.

E. Neis, *Erläuterungen zu Siegfried Lenz' Erzählungen*, Bange, Hollfeld/Obfr., 1972 (on seven stories from JdS., Fs.).

C. Russ, 'The Short Stories of Siegfried Lenz,' *German Life and Letters*, XIX (1965/6), 241–51. In German in *Siegfried Lenz: Ein Prospekt* and Russ, *Schriftsteller;* similar material in the afterword to the collected stories and the introduction to Russ's edition of *'Das Wrack'* and other stories.

C. Russ, 'The Macabre Festival. A Consideration of Six Stories by Siegfried Lenz,' in: *Deutung und Bedeutung, Studies . . . presented to Karl-Werner Maurer*, ed. B. Schludermann and others, Mouton, The Hague, 1973, pp. 275–93.

J.-J. Schuhmacher, 'Nouvelles de Siegfried Lenz. Du côté de chez Feddersen,' *Allemagnes d'aujourd'hui*, LVI (January-February 1977), 84–6.

J.-J. Schuhmacher, Review of *Einstein überquert die Elbe bei Hamburg*, *Allemagnes d'aujourd'hui*, LIX (September-October 1977), 91–3.

A. Schwenckendiek, 'Fünf moderne Satiren im Deutschunterricht,' *Der Deutschunterricht*, XVIII (1966), Nr. 3, 39–50 (pp. 45–7 on 'Lieblingsspeise der Hyänen').

B. Sowinski, 'Gruppenarbeit auf der Unterstufe, dargelegt am Beispiel von Siegfried Lenz' *Zirkus in Suleyken*,' *Der Deutschunterricht*, XXI (1969), Nr. 6, 38–44.

SELECT BIBLIOGRAPHY

Dramatic works

H. Beissel, 'Between Two Nightmares: The German Theatre after World War Two,' *Seminar,* I (1965), 55–68.

F. Bondy, 'Gericht über die Schuldlosen: oder, Die Szene wird zum Tribunal,' *Der Monat,* XIV (1961/2), 53–7.

H.-J. Greif, *Zum modernen Theater,* Bouvier, Bonn, 1973, pp. 65–75.

H.-J. Greif, 'Das szenische Werk' in: Schwarz, *Der Erzähler,* noted above under general studies.

H. Rischbieter and W. Wendt, 'Das totalitäre System "an sich": Siegfried Lenz,' in: *Deutsche Dramatik in Ost und West,* Friedrich, Velber bei Hannover, 1965, pp. 62–4.

H. Schwitzke, *Reclams Hörspielführer,* Reclam, Stuttgart, 1969, pp. 398–406.

III LENZ IN ENGLISH TRANSLATION

The Survivor (Stadtgespräch), tr. M. Bullock, Hill and Wang, New York, 1965.

The German Lesson, tr. E. Kaiser and E. Wilkins, McDonald, London, 1971.

An Exemplary Life, tr. D. Parmée, Secker, London, 1976.

The Lightship, tr. M. Bullock, Heinemann, London, 1964.

Lucas, Gentle Servant, tr. R. P. Heller in *German Narrative Prose,* ed. W. Rehfeld, Wolff, London, 1968, pp. 85–102.

Myself for Example, tr. E. Larsen in *Motives,* ed. R. Salis, Wolff, London, 1975, pp. 150–9.

6/1